MASTERING THE
BUSINESS OF PRACTICE

MASTERING THE BUSINESS OF PRACTICE

BY

MARC B. COOPER, DDS, MSD

The Mastery Company
Woodinville, Washington

MASTERING THE BUSINESS OF PRACTICE

Published by Sahalie Press
Woodinville, Washington
(425) 806-8830
metrix@emisar.com

ISBN: 978-0-9763584-0-4

Printed in the USA

Second Edition, 2009

Editing by Matthew King

Book design by Lightbourne, Inc.

THE MASTERY PROMISE

"Mastering your enemies makes you strong.
Mastering yourself makes you fearless."

— LAO TZU

In consulting a new client, my first step is to establish a clear definition of what it means to be successful. How would success look? How would it feel? How would you measure success? Who would you be that you're not now being if you were successful?

My personal definition of success in writing this book begins and ends with its impact on you. I'll consider it a triumph if it opens your eyes, engages your awareness and expands your understanding of yourself as an owner, manager, leader and marketer.

This was never intended to be a How-To book. This is a Who-To book. This volume is a mirror, in a way. Hold it up, look directly into your own eyes and fearlessly examine yourself and how you are running your practice as a business.

This book is presented in question and answer format. The questions come from clients and other dentists around the country. I selected each question in this book because I've run into it numerous times in more than two decades as a practice management consultant. They are questions I know you ask yourself — nearly every day.

My promise is a book that is eye-opening and energetic — one that will be ragged at the edges in five years. A book that impacts the way you run your practice as a business. A book true to the Mastery spirit and to those seeking to master the business of their practice. You have now taken the first step in your commitment to success.

Be fearless.

Marc B. Cooper, DDS, MSD

INTRODUCTION

What does it really take to have a highly successful practice?

You might think that having a thriving practice takes knowing the right way to run your practice as a business. And to run your practice as a highly profitable business, you might believe you must have precise scripts, the best business processes, and the most well-defined and highly calibrated systems. Sorry to disappoint you, none of these delivers success.

Practice success goes far beyond knowing *how to* produce the results. Practice success isn't the result of the right information, prescriptions, recipes, tips, and formulas. There is another domain to master without which success will not occur. And that is what this book is about.

This domain is about *who* you need to be as an owner, as a manager, as a leader and as a marketer. If you can't be a powerful owner, if you can't be an effective manager, if you can't be an inspirational leader, if you can't be someone who attracts patients, then whatever information you have and whatever actions you take will not be effective.

In order to access this domain of who you need to be in the practice, I have written this book using the most commonly asked questions culled from my 25 years as a practice management consultant.

By standing in the shoes of dentists who have asked these questions and by thoughtfully considering the responses, you will see yourself and how you are in your practice. You will see how the answers in this book teach profound lessons about yourself, which will allow you to change, resulting in you being more highly effective and powerful in your practice.

Lao Tzu once said; "Mastering your enemies makes you strong. Mastering yourself makes you fearless."

This book is about mastering yourself in the business of practice. This book will give you insights, revelations and a much deeper understanding of yourself as a leader, manager and owner. These insights will help you to think and act in new ways that allow you to produce much better outcomes and results.

This is your path to mastery. Let's take these first steps together.

Dr. Marc B. Cooper
The Mastery Company

FOREWORD

If you are reading this book, I hope you already know Dr. Marc Cooper. If you don't already know him and you are a dental practice owner, you will feel as if he knows you personally when you read this book. Really. Marc is as he claims to be: He knows the hearts and minds of dentists. Our thoughts and feelings apparently are quite universal, and, given that we generally all practice individually, we haven't yet appreciated how similar we are and how supportive we can be of one another. Marc is here to help, to make us successful business leaders, to increase our implicit and practical knowledge of management and to support us in creating futures.

As a dentist and dental practice owner of more than 20 years, I could have easily submitted all the questions that appear in this book, although I think I only really sent in one. And yet all these compressed, bite-size messages are concepts that I put into action almost immediately upon reading them, even if I didn't think that the particular issue was my most pressing concern. These messages un-bundle the management chaos that I often experience and divide heart-wrenching issues into do-able conversations and tasks. Voila! I am more genuine, content, creative and successful. Not that this doesn't take courage. But Marc encourages taking action even when our palms are sweating and our tummies are churning and our chests are tight. Yet physiologic responses are not the only indicators of change. I should let you know that when I follow Marc's advice, my practice numbers greatly exceed my targets and my staff reports increased contentment and success.

Marc Cooper is a pundit and a teacher. He makes you feel as if his knowledge becomes your own — a conjoined intelligence that elicits power and creativity. He helps you create a future without preconceived limits and he helps you to realize that living in the present does not need to be miserable — that you can "choose what you have chosen." Marc supports you in incubating and executing action plans that make your practice and patient care better. When you work with Marc, he demands that you never make promises lightly. He is a master at supporting you in relearning how your intuition is viable and valuable. And Marc lets you be astonished at yourself.

The information herein is more than just management vitamins, though. The messages cannot be read without creating change. Whether you are in a velvet rut or struggling to get by, these missives will help you create a future much better and different than the one you perceived yesterday. Your tomorrow will be quite different because of the message you took to heart and acted upon today. The brick wall in the way of solving that tricky staff issue now has a sparkling clear window to a potential solution. While in the past you may have felt dissatisfied but unable to describe what you wanted, you will now see that you can create a future of purpose and meaning.

Truly, what more could you ask for?

Dr. Sally Hewett
Family Practice
Chairman of Y.A.D.A. (Young Adult Dental Affiliates)
Bainbridge Island, WA

ACKNOWLEDGEMENTS

Roosevelt is quoted as saying,

"You alone must do it, but you can't do it alone."

For me, this is the essence of my work and this book. This book is the result of working with remarkable clients over the last 25 years. Professionals who hold me to account as their coach, their mentor, and their partner in success. In this kind of committed relationship, I am called upon to operate at my highest level and to continuously stretch myself to deliver consulting and coaching that strongly impacts and changes people. In essence, my clients wrote this book since my work has totally developed in service to them. I deeply acknowledge these clients who have allowed me to live my vision, serve my mission and stay on purpose. Without my relationship with my clients, this book would not have been possible.

Dr. Marc B. Cooper DDS, MSD
www.TheMasteryCompany.com
mcooper@emisar.com

DEDICATION

To my teachers, mentors and coaches; Charlie Smith, B. Braden, Werner Erhard, Alan Cahn, Herta Spencer, Mert Landay, Ron Bynum, Richard Condon, Harley Sullivan, Saul Schluger, Bill Ammons, Bob Hunter, and John Lohse. All of these individuals have enabled me to hold myself to my highest thought. They are professionals who believed in me, my work and who I am. And people in whose eyes I saw myself as who I wanted to be.

To Chris Creamer for his unconditional commitment, driving intention and gift of technology. Without Chris this book would never have been published.

DISCLAIMER

Results are a function of <u>integrity</u> and <u>structure</u>.

The information in this book can inform, coach and teach, but it cannot do it for you.

The information in this book cannot force you to operate with integrity.

The information in this book cannot give you the <u>courage</u> to confront problems with your partner or associate.

The information in this book cannot make you build and manage your <u>structures</u>.

It is up to you. You are responsible.   *You are the cause*

By responsibility, I mean that you see yourself as "<u>cause in</u> the matter."

Blame, shame, guilt and fault are the antithesis of responsibility.   *you are responsible*

No problem can be solved, no issue effectively handled, no concern effectively addressed, unless you hold that you are responsible.   *Do as/Be as one with*

Integrity is honoring your word as yourself.   *your words*

Integrity is making and keeping promises.

Integrity is holding yourself, each staff member and the practice accountable for its word.

So as you read this book and gain new knowledge and insights into your practice and yourself, remember: It is up to you to implement what you learn.

CONTENTS

LEADERSHIP

MANAGEMENT

MARKETING

THE MASTERY COMPANY

CONTEXT OF OWNERSHIP

OWNERS work "on" the business, not "in" the business. Ownership is the highest leveraged position of business, yet most dentists are unaware of how to be a powerful owner.

OWNERS have a limited number of rights given by law. Although those rights are limited in number, they allow owners to fully govern the business and permit them to command management and leadership.

OWNERS have the right to the distribution of the assets. Owners have the right to hire and fire. Owners have the right to sell the business. And — the most important of all — owners have the right to determine the future of the business.

OWNERS operate from a different temporality. Whereas management looks at today, ownership looks at the years ahead. Owners look outside of the business to see how it needs to be constituted to succeed, now and into the future. Owners look outside-in. Managers look inside-out.

OWNERSHIP'S JOB is to increase the value of the practice and to make sure it is worth more in the marketplace — its negotiable value

— each and every year. And the owner's job is to make sure the practice operates more effectively and efficiently — its operational value — every year. The owner must hire the right people to achieve those results and hold management and leadership accountable for producing them.

OWNERS need to be demanding, tough, rigorous and challenging. They need to hold people accountable. They need to demand unrelentingly that good enough is never good enough.

WHAT'S MISSING IS OWNERSHIP!

I have been in dental practice for 19 years and I just can't seem to get any traction on making money. I have a few good months, but then something always seems to go wrong — staff, number of new patients, equipment breakdown.

I keep up with CE, belong to great study clubs, study under restorative gurus, love the technical side of dentistry, enjoy my patients — and even like my staff most of the time. I read Dental Economics and Dental Town. I've hired consultants to help me improve my management and I've taken several leadership courses. I listen to audio tapes and read books on leadership and management and talk to colleagues about what they're doing. But every day I think about selling the practice and just going to work for someone else. I probably would make as much money without the headaches.

What's your advice?

• ◦ •

There are a number of things we could explore to find out why you aren't producing the revenue results you desire. According to your assessments, it seems that management is in decent shape. You love your dentistry and really care about it and you have had some training in leadership. So, I'd most likely begin with examining your performance as an *owner*.

Intention converts energy into results. It seems to me that you are lacking the most potent of intentions: the intention that owners bring to a business. Ask yourself this question:

"What would be missing from my practice if I took ownership out of it?"

I'd bet the ranch that nothing would be missing. You would still be there doing dentistry, the staff still there doing their jobs, the operations still going on. Nothing would be missing. You'd still be managing, you'd still be delivering care and you'd still be doing what you need to do to deliver that care. So "nothing" would be missing if I took ownership out of the practice because it wasn't there in the first place.

Many dentists haven't a clue about what ownership is or how to be an effective owner. Except for the Mastery Program, I know of no consultant, program, educational institution, book or article that teaches you about ownership. Where did you get your current knowledge and models on ownership anyway? Who taught you the way to own successfully? Answer: No one!

Ownership is not management. Ownership is not leadership. Ownership is its own domain with its own accountabilities, metrics, rights and privileges. Owners bring a potent, demanding, rigorous, driving intention to the business. Owners are the ones who are a constant, relentless demand for high performance and great customer care. Owners don't accept ineptitude from managers, staff or suppliers. Owners are about generating a successful business that delivers a strong return on investment.

Owners are tough. Owners are relentless. Owners are insistent. Owners operate out of a different temporality. Whereas managers think in hours and days, owners think in decades.

Let's say I gave you the ownership assignment of building a highly successful business that you could proudly give to your granddaughter. To do so, part of the assignment is to have the business generate $1.5M in revenues within three years. Your job is to have the business operate in such a way that employees get their jobs done impeccably, customers (patients) are fully served and the business runs on time and with an overhead of less than 50%.

Now let's say you put yourself on that track. There is no back door. It is either do or die. You would need to bring an unconditional commitment, a driving intention and take-no-prisoners attitude. If you would bring that approach to your practice, the perception and attitude of an owner, if you'd be an owner, your practice would operate differently and you'd make money.

So you need to change. You need to become tough, resilient, demanding. You need to make sure you and everyone else walk the talk. You have to be an owner and bring an owner's intention to the practice to have it perform so it generates the money you want. Are you up for that?

YOU DON'T KNOW YOU DON'T KNOW

Argggggghhhh! Managing staff! Worrying about the money! Being at the beck and call of patients and staff! All I want to do is do my dentistry.

I spend as much time in CE as possible. I travel to Seattle and spend time with a great teacher. After five years, I have achieved a level of competence in diagnosis, treatment planning and clinical delivery that is really strong. But I am struggling financially and have been ever since I began my practice.

I thought that if I achieved a level of distinction in my clinical dentistry, did beautiful work, was able to effectively diagnose, treatment plan and deliver top quality dentistry, I would be successful!

I can't even deliver what I know I can because I don't make enough money. I am forced to take third party payments in for the form of PPOs and other insurance plans just to stay busy. That means I write off about 20 to 30 percent of what I produce. Without a higher income and fee-for-service patients, I am forced to use cheap labs, and I can't afford a highly professional staff or top of the line equipment.

I have been blaming my struggles on my location, my staff, my market. Reading your e-letters, I'm beginning to think it might be me. What can I do?

• ○ •

Well clearly you don't know. In fact, you don't know that you don't know. You're deaf, dumb and blind to what really matters in being successful in dental practice. You can't see or understand why you're struggling. And you'll never solve the mystery of success simply by becoming a more able clinician.

What's the key to solving this mystery? The key is context. Context is decisive. Context rules. Context is superior ordinate. Context determines what succeeds and what fails. Context wins every time. Context is like gravity. No matter what you think when you jump out of the window, you're going to hit the ground. Context is crucial, the ultimate determinant.

The context of dental practice is "for-profit." The only thing that succeeds in a for-profit context is business. No matter how much you want your practice to be about excellence in dentistry, no matter how much you wish it could be about the most exquisite and latest techniques, no matter how much you crave to learn and use the latest and greatest materials, no matter how you yearn for dentistry to be about risk-assessment, veneers, implants, Invisalign or lasers — the success of a dental practice will always and ultimately be determined by how your practice is run as a "for-profit" business.

Make sense?

In a for-profit context the only thing that works is business. Business has requirements. Business has necessities. Business has invariant principles that must be followed. Business has personnel requirements that must be met. Business always requires leadership, management and ownership to work.

Business needs to figure out how to make money. Business needs to plan and execute so it makes more than it spends. Business needs to satisfy the needs of its workforce. Business needs to enable the owner to have a substantial return on investment. Business needs to provide products or services that people want and will pay for.

Business needs to allocate its assets, which includes cash, to continue to sustain the business infrastructure, people, materials and technologies that will meet the current and future wants and needs of the business and the market. And business needs to strategically think and act to fund the things that will have it succeed in the future.

If you don't like it that your practice is a business — too bad. Dental practice in the United States exists within a for-profit context. That's the way it is. Better accept it or sell your practice and go work for someone else, because that isn't going to change any time soon.

You've mastered the clinical side of practice. You can put on your clinician "hat" any time you want, and deliver great dentistry. You can put on your caregiver's hat and relate to your patients. But these two hats are woefully insufficient to run your practice as a business. You need a leadership hat, a management hat and an ownership hat. Then you need to know how and when to wear each of these hats.

I've been educating, training and developing dentists for more than two decades in leadership, management and ownership. To achieve ability in each of these domains, you must be willing and committed to going through the discomfort of traversing the arduous terrain of the "learning curve," especially the first leg of the climb. Then, when you finally learn what and how to be a leader, a manager and an owner, then you must practice and retain your discipline in each of these.

Context is decisive. Dental practices exist within a for-profit context. The only entity that survives in a for-profit context is a business. Without setting up your practice as business, you'll die. Context doesn't care. Context has no sympathy. Context has no compassion, kindness or empathy. It's simply a law of the universe. Abide by the law or perish.

What's missing for you? What's missing for you to be a driving commitment to master business? What's missing is possibility. What's missing is seeing the possibility that mastering business would give you. You hold business as a "have" to, not a "want" to, so you have no desire to master the elements that have business succeed.

In my view, mastering leadership, management and ownership gives you the possibility to succeed in every area of your life. So in my work, I see achieving business success as a means to an end. And that end is to be a more powerful, a more effective and more able human being who can now make a bigger difference not only with his or her patients, but also with their families, their communities and ultimately the world.

PERHAPS A LITTLE CHEESE WITH YOUR WHINE?

I have been in practice nine years in a suburban area of Philadelphia. I work hard, I take tremendous amounts of CE, I treat my patients like Kings and Queens, and I treat my staff like family. I hired the best interior designer to design my office. I hired a well respected marketing firm to do my Website, brochures, cards and Yellow Pages. I've done everything and anything to create a top-end practice, but I am just barely making it.

My competition appears to be doing a lot better. I struggle every month for new patients and production. This whole thing is a struggle. I feel helpless. What can I do?

• • •

You are not alone. I hear dentists all the time complain about how poorly their practices are performing in the area of revenues. Their complaints always come with stories, explanations, rationalizations and excuses such as;

> *I really take great care of my patients.*
>
> *I do excellent dentistry.*
>
> *Most of my patients don't have money and can't afford it.*
>
> *I live in a community that is insurance driven.*
>
> *I have a lot of competition.*

All these may be true, but so what? Your competition is kicking your butt and they practice in the same neighborhood. How do you explain that?

Your problem is you are not running your practice as a business. You are running your practice as a non-profit clinic and you have become a poorly paid salaried employee.

Given that you are in a for-profit business, when your practice is underperforming, the first place I'd suggest you look at is your integrity. Not moral integrity such as *He won't take a bribe.* No, I am speaking about business integrity. Those things that a business should do to give and keep its word as a business are not being done.

I promise you that it is invariant: the higher the business integrity the greater the revenues. The formula is proven, valid and unfailing.

Here is a list of questions to assess your business integrity. You should be asking yourself:

MONEY

Do I have a budget and am I strict and tough about spending — including staff salaries and benefits? Am I fully conscious about my money, not living in hope it will somehow all work out? Am I making more than I am spending? Am I able to generate a surplus or margin? If not, what specific actions do I need to do to accomplish this? Am I able to cover my bills without concern?

STAFF MANAGEMENT

Do I have performance criteria for staff and if they don't deliver, are there clear and understood consequences? Do I complete performance reviews routinely? Do I have a clear and fair raise policy? Do I recognize when I am acting like the benevolent parent, wanting to avoid conflicts or upsets? Do I have clearly defined job descriptions? Are these kept current?

GOALS & TARGETS

Do I have goals, not targets? What's the difference? Targets are what you want. Goals are what you can promise. Do I operate with my goals and press as hard as I can to make them happen? Do I recognize when I am resigned and, therefore, surrender and say I did the best I could? Is my staff's compensation tied to making these goals?

CORE VALUES

Have I clarified my core values? Do I make sure that the core values are adhered to and if not, are there defined consequences? Am I willing to fire someone who does not adhere to the core values? Do I walk the talk?

HONOR

Do I have real pride of ownership? Do I immediately intervene when my staff treats the practice like it's a "rental?" Do I speak about the practice with pride, admiration and deep respect?

VISION

Do I have a real vision? Do I see a future that I know is possible to achieve? Am I willing to be unconditionally committed to achieving this vision? Do I know when I am pretending that doing good dentistry is not nearly enough?

GOVERNANCE

Do I have well articulated governance policies and operational policies? Do I stick to these policies? If someone doesn't follow policy are there real penalties? Am I careful not to make decisions based on the moment, but based on well thought-out policies? Do I avoid executing policy because I know it will cause a breakdown and I'm scared to do that?

MARKETING

Do I deliver effective word of mouth marketing or is my marketing left up to external sources, such as Yellow Pages, radio spots and the Web? Do I realize when my basic marketing plan is just hope and prayer? Is marketing a daily activity? Do I have a metrics for marketing activity?

OWNERSHIP

Do I talk straight to my staff? Do I know when I am being nice and not direct? Do I know when I am wind-bagging? Do I make powerful and effective requests?

MISSION

Are we on a mission or is it business as usual? Is the mission real to me, my staff, and my market?

If you answered "No" to any of these questions, you need to convert them to a "Yes" in order to raise your level of integrity — the integrity of your practice as a business.

If you want to make money, run your practice as a business. If you just want to do dentistry, you're doing fine.

NO PURPOSE, NO SUCCE

I've just written my last check to a consultant. Third consultant in siʌ,
Each consultant has had me do a vision and mission. Same outcome. Nice
sounding words and no improvement in results.

What is going on!

•   ·   •

Every consultant has taken you through the process of developing a vision and mission statement. If that's all that was needed, a lot more dentists would be more successful. Unfortunately, many consultants don't get to the deeper and more profound core that gives power to a vision and muscle to a mission. Without this core, neither a vision nor a mission has much influence. What is this core? This core ultimately resides in who you are.

Without this powerful core, your vision and mission are hollow. No heart. No guts. No truth. Just well intentioned words such as, "My vision is to deliver quality care in an environment of comfort and service" and "We will be the premier restorative and cosmetic practice in our region."

You need to answer the most fundamental questions about yourself:

- Who am I really as a dentist and practice owner?

- What do I *really* stand for?

- Whom do I serve, *really*?

- Where am I *really* taking this practice?

- Where am I *really* going as a professional?

- Why does this practice *really* exist?

- What are my *real* core values?

- What are my true underlying philosophies?

If you can't answer these questions, your vision and your mission are both in jeopardy.

But when you can honestly answer these questions, your answers will reveal your purpose. A purpose is what you are unconditionally committed to. A purpose gives direction. A purpose orients your thoughts and actions. Covey, Dryer, Collins, Porter, Chopak, Drucker, Blanchard — all address the power of purpose in their work.

Your purpose is the reason for your existence. Your purpose is where you get your power from. Your purpose is what binds all the various parts of your practice — staff, decisions, systems, clinical processes — and directs them on the same path. Unfortunately, for most dentists, the purposes they profess are disingenuous.

A vision and mission coming from an inauthentic purpose will always lack authority. Is it any wonder why the staff isn't passionate about the practice? Without a higher purpose, the vision and mission are pretentious and hypocritical. Pretense and hypocrisy have no power.

Therefore, without a higher purpose your vision and mission lack integrity. You need to have a higher purpose other than your own success. And you need to be this higher purpose in being and action. You need to co-exist with this higher purpose.

A higher purpose has a noble principle. A higher purpose is honorable. A higher purpose is uplifting and virtuous. A higher purpose is about making a difference for others. A higher purpose aims to change the world for the better — to make it better for people. Without a higher purpose, the staff is only there for a job. Without a higher purpose the staff stays as an aggregate of individuals, not bound by anything except their individual motives.

A higher purpose focuses on the patients as human beings, how they will benefit, how their lives will be impacted. Therefore, your purpose must be a cause that will make the world a better place.

A higher purpose should take you beyond financial ambitions and feed your most profound ambition — to lead a meaningful life. Without a higher purpose your vision and mission are useless. Without a higher purpose your practice is simply an engine that provides dental services at a fair price.

Dentists who work with me know I reach deep down to have them find and operate out of their higher purpose. Because when they are "on purpose" they are powerful, fearless and commanding. When they are "on purpose" their vision and mission mean something.

MISSING: A PASSIONATE RELATIONSHIP

I have been in practice almost ten years. I love dentistry. I can't get enough CE. I take a ton of technical programs, study with master clinicians and read a bunch of journals. I spend hours on Dental Town reading about what other dentists are doing. With all the advances in dentistry, I am excited about all there is to learn.

But I don't have the same feeling about my practice. I don't like to manage staff. I don't like to look at my numbers. I don't like worrying about the bills, revenues, receivables, how many new patients, how many no-shows. I wish I could just do my dentistry and not have to worry about the practice.

Maybe that's why I am not financially successful. What should I do? Sell my practice and go to work for someone else? Maybe I'd do just as well without all the hassles.

• • •

Passion is the juice, the rocket-fuel that drives you to continuously push yourself to improve your knowledge and performance in clinical dentistry. OK, so you're passionate about what you're doing and what clinical outcomes you want to achieve as well as the kind of techniques you use. You're fanatical about improving your clinical skills using evolving methods and materials. You're obsessive about your continuing clinical education and totally captivated by your clinical gurus. Simply put, you are unconditionally and totally turned on about your dentistry.

At the same time this passion is totally lacking in the way you run your practice as a business. Running your practice as a business is a bother, a nuisance, a hassle. It's something you have to do, not what you want to do.

Without passion, there is hesitancy; there is refusal to push past your comfort zone. Without passion there is no creativity and a refusal to change course, learn new skills, abandon current practices or forge new directions. Without passion, there is a lack of courage and an unwillingness to be uncomfortable which breeds mediocrity and indifference.

16

passion ↔ commitment ⇄ action +
without vision → possibility
= disaster
in success

Marc B. Cooper, DDS, MSD

Passion is infectious. Passion delivers inspiration. Passion shrinks ego and displaces looking good. Passion motivates, provokes and enhances. Passion allows you to take risks. Passion opens you to coaching. Passion is what spurs success. People who are passionate about their business are successful in their business.

So why are you, someone who is so passionate about your technical skills, so dispassionate about the business of dentistry?

In order to have passion, a certain relationship must first exist with your practice. What needs to be present in this relationship that makes passion happen? First, the relationship must be driven by a strong intention to achieve an outcome. In your case, the only outcome you want to achieve from your practice is to give yourself a good job. That's not exactly what I would call a scintillating intention.

Second, the relationship must exist within a powerful vision of what you want to achieve in the future. You have a great vision about your clinical dentistry and zero vision about what you want to achieve with your business of dentistry. You could easily complete the statement, "The vision of my dentistry is [fill in the blank]. But you could not complete the statement, "The vision of my practice is [don't bother]. No vision, no possibility. No possibility, no commitment. No commitment, no effective action. If your relationship to your practice doesn't have possibility, commitment and vision, there won't be any passion either. I want to get pt excited at make through my doors to establish a community of pt who wants to create long lasting healthy better or smiles!

Third, in order to have passion the relationship must contain a compelling commitment to a mission. You have a mission for your clinical dentistry, but you have no mission for the business of your practice.

Bottom Line: In order to have passion, you need to have a relationship of loving what you do. This kind of relationship is missing between you and your practice. You tolerate your practice so you can do your dentistry. You're not alone. What's missing for most dentists is a true passion for the business side of practice, the overarching mission of the practice.

That might be why I am successful as a consultant. I am able to transform my clients' relationship to their practice from tolerant to passionate. How do I do that? Through my methods, I enable my dental clients see that

17

mastering the business of practice will not just give them financial peace of mind, but will enable them to grow and develop into the kind of person they have always envisioned themselves to be — powerful, courageous and effective. Mastering the business of practice will allow them to become strong leaders, potent managers and smart owners. With that possibility available, with good coaching, they begin to care for their practice rather than resent it. When their practice shows up as the vehicle for them to become the person they always wanted to be, they begin to love their practice.

WANTED: ONE 'GREAT' STAFF

I've been in practice for over 17 years and have never had a great staff. In fact I don't remember ever having a "good" staff. Out of the seven staff members I have now, there is only one I consider good — and that is my business manager who has been with me for eight years. I have always had a high turnover rate with assistants and front desk individuals, and the candidates I get are mediocre at best.

What do I need to do have a great staff?

• • •

First, and I don't mean to be harsh, but if you are like most dentists, you must realize you really don't care about having a great staff.

What you want is a staff that doesn't cause you any trouble, that is problem free, that does their jobs, doesn't ask for raises, comes to work on time and wants you to be financially successful. What you really want, what you are really looking for, is a "robo-staff," not a great staff.

If you really want a great staff, you need to think and act differently. Though this is very difficult, it can be done. There are four fundamental domains that need to significantly change for you to have a great staff: ownership, leadership, management and hiring the right people.

In the domain of ownership, nearly every dentist has it totally wrong. Nearly all dentists own a practice to make lots of money, provide themselves with a good job and have a profession that is fairly secure against economic downturns. Few, if any, dentists build a dental practice to generate a "great" business.

Let me say it again: Few, if any, dentists build a practice to generate a great business, a business that will succeed them, that will continue to grow and expand, that will become something unique and special. There aren't any Intels, Microsofts or IBMs in dentistry. Nearly every dentist owns a practice to give him or herself a good job, not to build a great business. And that is a major barrier to generating a great staff.

19

Why? When you own a practice to give yourself a great job and make lots of money, you own a business based on the context of "I" and not "we." And as I always say, "Context is decisive." You simply can't build a great team within the context of "I."

When you think and act from the context of "I" and not "we," you automatically build in a barrier to attracting, recruiting and retaining great staff. How many dentists have you ever met with a driving commitment to developing great staff members, paying them lots of money and enabling them to reach higher and higher levels of professional and personal development? I don't think many. Why? That commitment can't live in the context of "I." And without that commitment, how can you attract and retain great staff?

The context of "I" is so strong in dentistry that nearly 90 percent of all dentistry consists of solo practices. It also explains why 80 percent of dental partnerships fail. The context of "I" forces dentists to hire staff that must keep him or her as the lead dog. And you know what they say about the view when you're not the lead dog. It's always the same.

What dentists do is try to hire a crew of highly capable helpers to make their practices work. This way they can make lots of money; they can have a good job for a long time and they can be in a profession that is economically stable. That might explain why there are so few really outstanding individuals for hire in dentistry — individuals who want to be more than good helpers, professionals who want to make a difference, who want to be accountable and who want to be leaders in their own right. Those kinds of opportunities simply aren't available in dentistry.

The first change required to have a great staff is you changing as an owner. You need to begin looking at building your practice as a great business, not a small business where you continually take all the money out of the top drawer.

NO MORE SURPRISES!

I have been in practice 18 years. I have used practice management consultants over the years to try to handle a recurring and very bothersome problem: Surprises.

For instance, last week I found out my schedule wasn't full for more than one week out when I was walking around thinking I was booked 3-4 weeks ahead. The only reason I found out was because I had to reschedule a study club meeting and needed to put the new date on next month's schedule.

Another example took place seven months ago when I went to the ATM to take out some cash only to find out how little money was in the checking account on the 20th of the month. I thought it would be around $30,000 and it turned out to be $11,000. I didn't even know I had a collection problem. Another surprise. And just this morning, I found out about two patients I presented large cases to that I thought were scheduled for treatment but who ended up canceling and not returning. The only reason I found out about them was I happened to be thinking about them driving to work and I asked my front desk about them when I got in. Another surprise.

I hate surprises. Why doesn't the staff bring such issues to my attention in a timely fashion? Why am I the last to know?

•　•　•

In the corporate world they use the word "culture," the conditions in which the business operates. Another way to say it is that the culture is the context within which the company exists. Culture — context or condition — is decisive. Air to the bird, water to the fish, culture to a business. Every business, whether large or small, has a particular culture. Bottom Line: You need to change your culture.

If you changed your culture, you would eliminate surprises and you would have a staff that keeps you fully informed. To achieve this you would need to generate a culture in which only the facts and the evidence drive decision making. You could control surprises if you built a culture where telling the truth and admitting mistakes was a requirement for yourself and every staff member. For most dentists, however, that would be a monumental task.

The current culture of most practices results in dentists not knowing what is going on inside their practices — making effective management impossible. In most practices, staff members deliver only good news to the dentist. A significant contributing factor to that culture of pretense is a dentist who is complicit in his or her own deception; he or she only wants to hear good news, even if it isn't the truth! Dentists want to hear that everything is on track so they can relax and feel good.

If your staff tells you bad news, you've got to deal with a serious problem. First, they don't know how to fix the problem. Why else would they be telling you? So now you face not only the hard work of helping them solve the problem, but also the grim prospect of facing the breakdowns that the problem has caused.

Dentists avoid the nitty-gritty reality. I find it common that dentists embrace a comfortable distance from the numbers and the facts about their practices. They prefer to live in La-La Land, preferring to hear how good everything is. Dentists actually give off signals that they don't want the truth.

You have your work cut out for you: to build a culture within your practice where telling the truth is accepted and expected. If you generate such a culture, you could address problems before they become too severe and make decisions based on the data and not some fantasy. But that is easier said than done.

Your first step, which is the hardest, is to drive fear out of the practice. When I consulted a Fortune 500 technology company a few years ago, I experienced something I have never seen in dentistry. This company's culture encouraged "constructive confrontation," where managers were encouraged to disagree and present alternative data and viewpoints to ensure better decisions. That was the company's way of requiring leadership to show employees that they didn't have to be afraid of telling the truth and openly admitting their mistakes.

Your second step is to create a practice culture where people are not afraid to ask for help. You'll have to give up your "I'm too busy and I'm overwhelmed" act, which naturally pushes staff away and implicitly warns them not to ask for help. You'll need to continuously tell your staff it is no sin to admit difficulty and to call in reinforcements. And make it just as clear that if a staff person tries to bluff his or her way out of trouble, it will result in termination.

At staff meetings, you need to constantly ask, "What might go wrong? What isn't working? What are the problems? And what keeps you/them up at night?" You are not doing that to catch them, to be negative or critical. You are doing it to plan and take action for issues and problems — good, bad and downright ugly.

And lastly, you yourself will need to change. Your current relationship to bad news is to remain as unconscious as possible until the wheels fall off. You think that if you don't know, it can't or won't happen. Denial doesn't work — period.

If and when you change your relationship to bad news, you can build a culture in which people are rewarded for identifying problems. My experience as a consultant is the more a practice — or any business for that matter — is able to put the brutal reality on the table and confront the real facts and issues, the more successful it will be.

Most dentists want to hear only the good news. That's BAD news! It pushes staff to fudge and equivocate. Want to succeed? Insist on the cold, hard facts.

YOU DON'T HAVE TO BE RAMBO TO TACKLE OWNERSHIP

I just read your newsletter about ownership. I have NEVER heard anyone talk about ownership in dental practice before. I found it very interesting — and disturbing.

In my heart I believe you are right on the money. For some reason, though, this scares me. Words like "tough, resilient, demanding" don't describe me. "Easygoing" maybe, "unassuming" maybe, "softie" maybe — but certainly not "tough, resilient or demanding." So that leaves me wondering. If I need to become someone I am not in order to be a successful business owner, perhaps I have no business owning a dental practice.

It sounds to me like I would have to adopt a very different persona and maintain that 24/7 to be a successful owner. And, you know, I could probably do that for a while. But the energy required to do so would wear me down eventually.

I'm not looking for a quick fix or something that necessitates that I become someone I'm not. I'm looking for sustainable, realistic, long-term results.

Your advice?

· ◦ ·

Ownership is a way of being. It is not an all-or-nothing phenomenon. I know that there have been times in your life when you have been a powerful owner — times when you have been "resilient, demanding and tough." So ownership is something you already have, but more than likely are not expressing consistently.

Ownership is in every one of us. It is just a matter of manifesting it. Unfortunately, like most dentists, you have no idea where the levers and dials are located to turn ownership on and off. I am very familiar with that blindness because one of my jobs is to enable dentists to know where, when and how to be an owner.

Ownership isn't exotic, esoteric or unique. I can promise you if you are committed, if you are highly intended, if you care enough about creating a great practice, you can be a powerful owner.

Every day you put on the hat of professional caregiver when you walk into the operatory. You have no problem shifting to that way of being. In fact, it's easy for you to do. But if you recall, it wasn't at all easy when you started your training. Remember your first patient in dental school?

Then, after you had been in practice for a while, you found models and mentors and developed yourself as a leader. You generated a vision, you captured a mission and you were on purpose. You learned to put on the leadership hat, and more than likely you now wear it well — with your staff, your patients and even your colleagues. You put on that hat and can you step out and align your staff, get them to go in the same direction and get them inspired by what the practice can deliver. That's being a leader.

And if you're like most practitioners, you also had to learn to wear the hat of manager: interacting with your staff to produce results, setting goals and targets, setting up systems and structures, convening morning huddles, etc.

You have learned over time and through experience how to be a professional care deliverer, a leader and a manager. Ownership is simply one more hat to master. But ownership will be the most difficult of all to achieve. Why? It is the one that is the least egocentric and requires the most courage.

Ownership has to do with building a successful business, not giving yourself a great job. Ownership is about building a legacy, not funding your retirement. Ownership is about developing the practice for transition, not making it easy on you. Ownership is about tomorrow, not today.

In my view, most dentists are weak owners because they put themselves ahead of their businesses. Look at how most dentists manage their finances. They take as much out of the top drawer as they can. How much do they reinvest into their businesses so they're built to last? How much do they invest in their staffs to create loyalty, high performance and longevity?

When you become a powerful owner, your focus is on building a great practice. Your intent is on something bigger than you. Your commitment is to drive the practice to perform at its top level, to never give up, to never believe that good enough is good enough. Management doesn't do that. It is focused on the day-to-day. Leadership doesn't do that. It is busy generating a vision and inspiring people. Caregivers don't do that. They are in service and need to be wholly compassionate. That leaves the tough work up to ownership.

So ownership is already part of your being and you need to understand it and wear the hat when required. But you don't need to wear the hat all the time. Just as you change hats from caregiver to manager to leader, shifting back and forth, now all you need to do is put on the hat with the big "O" on the front at the appropriate time, in the appropriate place and with the appropriate people — and exercise your rights and power as an owner.

I'M DOING SO WELL,
WHY AM I WORRIED?

I am a 45-year-old general practitioner. I have one of the more successful practices in my area. I am doing a little over $1.3 million a year in revenues. I have a good staff. I have a great associate who will make a good partner. I stay on the leading edge of dentistry, train with top flight clinicians and have an office that would knock your socks off.

But when I am all alone, when I am by myself, I am scared that I won't continue to succeed. I'm afraid I'll lose my edge, desire and drive. Part of the fear is I have no idea where to go from here. How do I continue to grow and manage a much larger practice? All I can see in front of me is a ton more work, less time and more hassles — which isn't very motivating. I have talked to some consulting groups that specialize in transitions and practice management and my feeling is they don't have any better idea than I do. They offered one of their prepackaged programs for $30K to $50K. Been there and done that — it just doesn't feel like a fit. So I thought I'd write and see what you have to say.

What can I do?

• ◦ •

Like many dentists, you are having a very difficult time surviving your success.

Initially, it was "Can I make it?" And soon that question was answered. Then, it was "Can I move from the back of the pack to the middle?" And, within two to three years you nailed that challenge.

Then, during your next five- to ten-year stretch, there was "Can I move to the front of the pack?" Lo and behold, soon you sat in the top ten percent of practices, with revenues over $1.3 M, a personal income of about $500K, a staff of around eight or nine with two or three seasoned veterans, a young and eager associate and this feeling that you have no idea what's next or how to continue your success.

During your rise to glory, the primary objective was to be better than others. To be better than others meant mastering the steps along the path that other dentists take. By using CE, advisors, consultants, study clubs, journals and many other resources, you clawed and scrambled your way to the top of the heap. And you are left with the question, "Now what?"

Indeed, now what will you do? You realize that doing the same things other dentists do — only more, better or different — isn't going to enable you to continue your success. You have used up the future available to most dentists.

Dentists are trained and cultured not to think for themselves. They are developed through competition with colleagues and that's the way they practice. They are developed in the ancient Japanese tradition of growing taller by cutting off the heads of those around them. They succeed by becoming better at the same things that other dentists do. That's where you now find yourself. But being better than other dentists has no more juice left for you. There ain't no gold left in that vein. You've mined it clean.

My solution, one that has been successfully delivered over the last ten years with many dentists like yourself, is to shift the context of your practice.

In my corporate consulting experience, well-managed corporate entities produce high quality, high service, high performance and high revenues. When I work with dentists like you, we work together to transform their practices. We do so by applying the principles of information, knowledge and wisdom of successful mid-sized and large corporations to dental practices.

These practices operate on totally different principles, structures, management, vision, mission and purpose than other dental practices. They use models, structures, and accountabilities of successful corporate entities as the developmental ladder.

We convert styles of leadership and management to operate on a corporate level. For example, we develop a senior executive team. We educate, train and develop select staff to be senior executives so we can have the functions of CFOs, HR directors, COOs and VPs of Marketing. We train the senior dentist to think and act like a CEO. Eventually, we put together a Board of Directors using outside already-successful professionals who operate as a governing board — defining the ends, generating effective policy, continuously enhancing the vision and being responsible for the success of the strategic plan. In essence, we transform a dental practice from a small business to a corporate business.

Here's my recommendation: *Commit to creating such a practice* — where the gap is deep and wide, where the risks are high, and where the challenges are great. Where courage, greatness and vision are required. Where you don't know how to do it — but you do know you will do it.

My experience with successful dentists who have reached the top ranks convinces me that you will continue your success if you take the leap to a new context of generating a corporate practice.

MEASURE. MEASURE. MEASURE!

*I am a general practitioner with a staff of eight. I've been in practice
20-plus years. I've never been able to get a good handle on managing
my staff. I am so busy with patients and clinical care I have no time for
management. So I rely on my office manager to manage staff. But she is
managing the front desk tasks, collections and recall and doesn't have time
to manage the staff either.*

*Basically, the only time I manage staff is when there is a problem and then
it's usually too little too late.*

What should I do?

• ∙ •

Measure!

That's right, measure!

Why? Because you can only manage what you measure. So I strongly
suggest you consider applying measurement to staff performance, staff
relations and staff attitude.

When I was learning my trade, I worked for three well-established
consulting companies: JMJ, Producere, and Charles Smith & Associates.
The clients of those consulting enterprises were Fortune 500 companies
— GE Capital, Boeing, Intel, Royal Dutch Shell and others. All three of
these enterprises used surveys and assessments during their engagements.
Customer Satisfaction. Employee Satisfaction. 360s. Meyers-Briggs. The
Enneagram.

Why did they use these tools? Because it allowed them to effectively
measure critical and fundamental areas of the client company so they
could know what was working and what was not working in their
organizations. Like good medicine or dentistry, the consultants I learned
from knew they couldn't design a good "treatment plan" without an
accurate "diagnosis." Scientifically valid, well-proven surveys give you that
diagnostic information.

We have adopted that same principle in our practice management work. We use a number of surveys and performance assessments that effectively measure staff performance, staff inter-relations and staff attitude. The surveys reveal how staff members feel about their work, about the practice, about each other and about the dentist. We also use performance reviews to evaluate the performance and results of each staff member. In other words, we educate and train dentists to measure, measure and measure some more, so they have a constant and accurate measure of the pulse of the staff.

We strongly recommend our practice management clients use surveys that ask the right questions about what is important in keeping a staff satisfied and productive. Questions that are scientifically valid and focus attention on areas fundamental and critical to staff fulfillment and performance.

So I suggest you use survey instruments that assess your staff members so you know what is going on with them. We have developed our own assessments, but there are other companies that deliver useful instruments such as Press-Ganey and Gallup. I am little prejudiced about our tools because they are especially designed for dentists, by dentists. And they are less expensive. But choose the one that works best for your practice and start measuring.

When you measure something, you focus on it — and that forces you to manage it.

THE POWER AND PITFALLS OF GOALS

I've only been in practice a few years. My peers and the practice management CE programs and books I've read all say to set goals. Well, I have. I set production and collection goals, new patient goals, and even spending limit goals. The problem is I never make my goals.

Since I never make my goals, I stop paying attention to them and just hope I make enough to cover costs and salaries. When I don't make my goals I get depressed and it makes me feel miserable and I feel like a failure.

I know I should set and use goals, but every time I do, it doesn't work for me. What should I do?

• ◦ •

You are confused about goals. The way you hold goals is totally disempowering rather than empowering.

You need to realize that goals are "man-made," they do not exist in nature. My dogs do not have goals. Goals are a human invention. Since you invent goals, why not invent them so they give you power, confidence and results. Why invent them so they make you feel bad, trash your self-worth, and keep you from making money?

Goals have no intrinsic meaning. You invest meaning into them. So the question becomes what meaning do you give your goals? More than likely you look at your goals as if they mean something about "you." Goals are supposed to be something you "have." But to you, goals are something you "are." By holding goals as something you are, this translates into "*When goals are met, who you are is good and when goals are not met, who you are is inadequate and bad.*"

You need to understand that goals have no inherent meaning. It's you that provides meaning to them. Goals don't come with a built in guarantee that you'll benefit by reaching them or enjoy the process of getting there. They don't even assure you're on the right track. Goals don't require inspiration, they require perspiration. Goals by their nature require a down-to-earth, pragmatic effort of getting things done.

Goals make you measure. Goals, therefore, are used to measure practice performance. Keeping score gives you feedback. You cannot change, adapt or improve without feedback. Numbers are unbiased. Numbers don't care. Measurements give you information on what outcomes you are producing from the actions you are taking. Numbers inform you when to adjust or change. Numbers tell you if it worked or not.

The problem is that dentists love to keep score as long as they're winning. When they're not winning, they don't want to see the report card. Like you, when dentists see a poor number, they make it mean something about them. They take it personally. They prefer to act on things they think are great and allow themselves to be misled, rather than pay attention to the evidence (numbers) and take appropriate action.

I use goals for several reasons with my clients. First, I use goals to "keep the end in mind." Steven Covey in his book, *The 8th Habit*, says to start all things with the end in mind. The challenge for many of my clients is to define which end to keep in mind. In Covey's view, this end is not an overarching numerical outcome or a destination, but "it's a way of life to which we should aspire." Set your goals to keep you operating in a manner that reinforces you to "live the life to which you aspire."

On a more pragmatic side, I coach my clients to use goals as a powerful way to hold their commitments in place and keep their commitments in front of them. In my consulting jargon, I call this a "structure of existence." Goals hold commitments in existence. Without an existence structure, commitments disappear. Setting goals constantly reminds and reinforces the commitments you made. Therefore, goals keep your attention and intention on fulfilling your commitments.

Goals allow you to operate with and inside integrity. My definition of integrity is when your words, actions and intentions all line up. So in this regard, a goal is a promise. A promise is giving your word to a future. To make the goal you need to operate (action) as your word. When you act as your word, you significantly reduce subjective analysis, psychology, excuses, stories, explanations, complaints, assessments, and what I call "trivial pursuit."

Results are a function of integrity and structure. Goals fully embody these two elements: integrity and structure. Goals push you to give your word and keep it — integrity. And goals are physical and tangible — a structure. Therefore, goals enhance your capacity to produce results.

If I were coaching you I'd ask you to make goals that are not a sure thing, but are not pie-in-the-sky either. I would ask you to create goals that you feel are really possible — goals that you could honestly commit to achieving. And then we'd work on the "who, how and when" to make these goals. I'd hold you to your word and make sure your actions and intentions lined up with you word.

For me goals are simply a tool, like a hammer or a screwdriver. Nothing more. If you don't make your goals about you, but make goals simply a tool for your practice, you'll be able to use goals to build a successful practice.

SETTING YOUR PRACTICE GOALS

I'm sitting at my desk setting my goals for next year. I do this every year.

How I set my goals is I figure a 10% increase over the last year. I pick 10% because that's what the experts say. The way it works is I take last year's numbers, look to see what I should do with about a 10% increase across the board, further break it down to how many patients I'll need to do that, how much restorative, hygiene and so forth. Then I look at my calendar, look at the number of days I am going to work and figure what I need in production per day. Then I figure out my monthly targets from all that.

Is this the right way to set my goals? Since I never make my goals, am I doing something wrong?

• • •

First of all, you are not establishing goals, you are setting targets. There is a big difference between a goal and a target. The difference between goal and a target is a target is something you "want," whereas a goal is something you are "committed to."

Targets are something you want to achieve. Targets are what you hope you will do. Targets are past-based. Targets are what you think you are supposed to do. But targets lack power. Targets don't really influence action. And in most cases targets turn out to be just a pipe dream.

When I speak with my clients around their future numbers, I have tough and rigorous interactions. I ask them, "Can you promise these results?" "Is it something you want or is it something you are willing to give your word to?"

Targets are like New Years resolutions. They are things you feel like you should and want to achieve. But two weeks after December 31st, they turn out to be just good ideas. "I'll get in shape. Go to the gym. Diet. Fully fund my retirement. Spend more time with my kids. Be more attentive to my spouse. Get my paper work done on time." And so it goes.

A commitment transforms a promise into reality. Commitments are words that speak boldly of your intentions and the actions which speak louder than your words. A commitment is making the time when there is none, coming through time after time, year after year. Ultimately, commitment is the stuff character is made of, the power to make things happen.

I don't think you need to change your model of goal setting. I think you need to change yourself. I think you need to commit. The problem is most dentists don't understand commitment. They don't know that a commitment is a relationship-based phenomenon. In other words, a commitment made to yourself rarely ever happens. A commitment made to another has a much greater chance of being achieved.

The odds are you are practicing solo, so you have no "committed listener" to your commitments. It's very easy to let yourself off the hook. Easy to say something got in the way. Easy to make up a story why you don't or can't get it done. Easy to make excuses. And since you're the boss and sign the pay checks, who's going to hold you to account. Nobody!

Between 1991 and 1997, I did a fair amount of corporate consulting. I consulted with executives of some large companies and a few Fortune 500s.

The executives in these billion-dollar companies weren't any smarter than the dentists I work with. They had all their frailties as human beings. Their cultures were not all that much better than many dental practices. People still moaned and groaned, gossiped and complained. They had staff problems, equipment breakdowns, new technology challenges, cash flow issues, receivables to manage. You get the picture. But what they had that most dentists don't have is someone they reported to: a committed listener. Someone who held them to account. Someone who held them rigorously to their word. And the frequency of these executives making and keeping commitments was significantly better than many dentists.

Don't tell anyone, but that's the secret of my consulting success. Simply put, I am a committed listener for my clients and I hold them to account for giving and keeping their word. It's no wonder my clients achieve their goals. Commitment produces effective action. Effective action produces results. Commitment shows up in your checkbook and calendar. Commitment means you get it done by when you say you'll get it done. And the likelihood of a commitment being fulfilled is dramatically enhanced by having a committed listener.

Find yourself a committed listener. Make promises about what you'll achieve next year. Give the committed listener permission to hold you to account and the likelihood of you achieving your goals will increase significantly.

SETTING YOUR PRACTICE GOALS (ADDENDUM)

Your last newsletter was great. I suggest you follow it with a piece on structures for commitment. All the commitment in the world will not necessarily create results without good structures (planning, metrics, measurement, monitoring and control).

This was a fundamental flaw my last company fell into over and over again. Whenever we ran into performance problems, we just tried to be more committed. It was only when the structures matched the commitment that we really produced.

— Art Haines

• • •

You are "dead on." Results are a function of two distinct yet highly related elements, commitment and structure.

Clearly commitment is fundamental. By commitment we mean the unconditional intention to give your word and keep it. Conducting yourself from your promises, not your circumstances. Unreservedly acting as your word, not your feelings. No excuses. No reasons. No justification. No explanations. Who you are is your word!

But commitment will not do it alone. Commitment wilts without structure. Commitment unravels without structure. So you need to build two kinds of structures to hold your commitment in place and, therefore, enable your commitment to be accomplished. Around each commitment you need to construct a structure of existence and develop and maintain a structure for fulfillment.

Structures of existence are physical manifestations of commitment. Such structures include explicit plans anchored to unambiguous milestones and defined dates when these milestones will be achieved. "I'm committed to increasing new patients by 30 percent next year," won't occur without, "We will ask a minimum of four patients per day to refer a coworker, family member or friend. We will check and make sure we did this at every morning huddle. And we will monitor our effectiveness by measuring where new patients come from on a daily basis."

By generating a structure for existence, the commitment is brought present in a physical form. It is held in place by daily activities, activities that are tangible and measurable. The commitment is pounded into your reality by having it manifested as actionable, measurable and frequent activities, documents and displays.

If you want to find out what a practice is truly committed to, see what structures of existence are present. If the commitment is not in some physical form, one that is looked at every day and talked about every day, then the commitment really doesn't have any punch.

When I first speak to potential clients about their overhead, they invariable say they want their overhead at 50%. But when I ask to see their budget and their budget targets for their variable expenses for that month, talk about your deer in the headlights. Or when I ask about what they want to produce in revenues per month, they always have a figure in mind. But when I ask them to show me their written goals (yearly, monthly, weekly and daily), their daily tracking mechanism, and their agendas for their morning huddle? Talk about your good intentions!

If a commitment lacks a real, tangible, measurable structure, if a commitment doesn't have a physical form that people can witness, it's not going to happen. Now it's pretty understandable why people don't embody their commitments in a structure for existence. Because once you put the commitment into existence, you put yourself at stake at making it happen. A structure of existence tells the world, here is my commitment in a form you can see, feel and touch. Putting your commitment in this kind of structure puts you on the hook.

The other structure that holds a commitment in place is a structure of fulfillment. A commitment made to yourself is basically a New Year's resolution. A commitment made to yourself has a very short shelf life. These kinds of commitments become extinct quickly. It's only when you make a commitment to another, someone who will hold you to account to achieve this commitment, is the commitment likely to happen.

Being willing to make your promise to another (or others), someone who is willing to hold you to account for your promise, will keep the commitment alive and make that promise real. So to fulfill your promise, you need another or others who will hold your "feet to the fire" to keep your word. These structures for fulfillment, having a person who will hold you to your commitment, are missing in most dental practices. Since most dentists practice solo, they don't have someone they entrust to hold them to their word.

In my consulting, I push my clients hard to build their structures of existence and I serve as a structure for fulfillment for their commitments. It's the basic model of my consulting practice, commitment, structures of existence and structure for fulfillment. That's why my clients produce results time and after time, year after year. It's not magic. It's simply a model that works.

YOUR RELATIONSHIP TO FAILURE NEEDS IMPROVEMENT

I've only been in practice four years and I feel like I'm failing. Two of my staff just quit. I haven't made my revenue goals or new patient goals in six months. Three new dentists just moved into my neighborhood. And some of my dentistry hasn't been that successful either. I am in a terrible mood. It's affecting my marriage and my health. I feel like giving up.

Some really successful dentists I know look like they have never really struggled. They seem to have the magic touch. And when I get with them at our study club, they talk about being successful like it's absolutely no sweat, which only makes me feel worse.

I hired a consultant. She is giving me advice about trying positive thinking, about trying to change my attitude. But it's just not working. In fact, it is making me feel worse.

What can I do?

• ◦ •

You can't succeed without failing. No one, and I mean no one, succeeds right out of the box. What needs to be altered is your relationship with failure.

In 1983 I was training to be a seminar leader for Landmark Educational Corporation. In the beginning, I was failing miserably. One of our leaders, Randy sent me a short, little story that I'll share with you.

> *There is the story of the young fellow who asked a bearded sage he met on the path, "Which way is success?" The weathered monk said nothing and gestured down the path. The young seeker was elated, and rushed ahead.*

> *Suddenly, there came the sound of a splat. In a little while, the seeker, now tattered and stunned, limped back, assuming he must have taken a wrong turn. He repeated his question to the monk, who again pointed silently in the same direction.*

41

The seeker nodded and turned, and headed back in the same direction as before. This time the sound of the splat was deafening. When the seeker crawled back, he was bloody, broken and very angry. Screaming at the monk, he demanded to know why he was sent off in the direction of disaster. "No more pointing, talk!"

Only then did the sage speak. "Success is that way," he said. "Just a little past the splat."

Every dentist with whom I have ever worked, who has achieved enduring success, has suffered a pile of embarrassments and stunning defeats. They all have a huge portfolio of mistakes they made. Yes, life is short, but some days are very long.

You are way off base crediting highly successful dentists with super human attributes, putting them on a pedestal. Unfortunately, many of these highly successful folks may pretend they've made few mistakes, rarely admitting their failures. But fear not, they are just like you.

Like you, successful dentists also face life-long adversity, phobias and flaws that they will never overcome. The only difference is they find a way to manage them. Somehow they refuse to let their vision and goals be held captive by their feelings in that awful moment when everything has gone wrong.

I understand and appreciate that you have a received a body blow from which you are now in shock. The shock will last for a while. But soon you will move through the various stages of recovery: from hurt, to guilt, to anger, to recovery. With my clients, I refuse to buy into their emotional response and I ask them to come clean; to fully acknowledge their pain and their breakdown; to take full responsibility for their situation.

It is only when you can accept responsibility that you can begin to take actions that will make a difference. It's only when you are responsible that you can learn from your breakdowns. It's only when you are responsible that you can generate authentic commitments which lead to effective action.

Now I know that some consultants suggest you use positive thinking. "Keep a positive attitude," they recommend. I haven't met very many dentists who can keep a positive attitude when they have a major setback. In fact, for most of my clients, it really hurts.

But what makes highly successful dentists different from others is they are able to avoid being stuck in negative emotions. They are able to move quickly to committed action. It's what you choose to do rather than how you feel about it that makes the difference.

I don't coach my clients to feel good when bad things happen. I have never been able to find the switch that magically allows them to think positively when things go wrong. And as you have experienced, thinking they should be able to think positively doesn't help. It only makes them feel worse.

My job as their coach is to have them deal with it directly, instead of trying to put a smile on their face. I don't want them to pretend to be happy when things go wrong and, at the same time, I instill in them an attitude where they refuse to surrender to their current disappointment.

Desmond TuTu, the Noble Peace Prize-winning archbishop, once said, "It's natural to feel like hell when things turn out badly. But don't let that stop you. Emotions are a storm that sweeps through your life. The defeat you've had matters less than what you ultimately want to create." And I have found that just like a storm, emotions too shall pass.

Successful dentists feel the pain, but they cherish what they're building more than the misery of the moment. Instead of struggling to fix their attitude, highly successful dentists don't worry about choosing their attitude, they shift their focus to what works and when they do that, their attitude improves as well.

In the words of Samuel Smiles:

> *It is a mistake to suppose that men succeed through success; they much oftener succeed through failures. Precept, study, advice, and example could never have taught them so well as failure has done.*

BE ACCOUNTABLE

I must be nuts. Every time there is a staff problem or staff issue, I automatically think that it will work out.

I have a situation now with a long term (eight years) employee who until recently was great. But for the last six months she has had pressing family issues, which have totally changed her performance and her mood. She's now infecting the entire staff.

But as usual, I just come to work, hoping it will fix itself.

What's wrong with me?

• • •

There is nothing "wrong" with you. You are like most dentists. You hate confrontations, so you avoid them. You can't stand putting yourself at risk, so you don't. You don't like being in uncomfortable situations, so you keep away from them. So you stick your head in the sand and hope for the best.

The question isn't how to fix you. You don't need fixing. The question is what structures do you need that would push you past your discomfort, past your fears, and past your unwillingness to take a risk?

When I consult in the corporate environment, I encounter the same human reaction by senior executives in confronting their down-line managers and supervisors. These executives want to avoid confrontations, stay away from uncomfortable situations, and just be left alone to do their work. Sound familiar? But in a corporate culture there is a structure in place that pushes them to act. That structure is accountability. And that's what's missing in your dental practice. There's no accountability.

You see accountability could be defined as "what you can be counted on for." As the owner, senior manager and leader, you are accountable for staff performance, staff relations and staff behavior. In this domain, you are the bottom line. And as the accountable party, you should handle your staff issues directly, powerfully and completely.

44

But accountability is a relationship-based phenomenon. You have to be accountable to someone and there is no one you are accountable to. There is no one who holds you to account for staff performance and staff relations. With no one holding you to account, you simply let yourself off the hook.

You make excuses. "I don't have the time. It'll work itself out. If I speak with her it will cause a mess. Next week will be better." You know, those hundreds of excuses, justifications and reasons you say to yourself every day.

But if you were in a corporate environment, you would have to report to someone who would hold you to account. Someone who would hold you to your word. Someone who would demand you have your people perform. Someone who wouldn't tolerate you being a chicken. And inside that relationship of accountability, you would put your fears aside and step in.

This is one of my primary functions as a consultant. It's what distinguishes me from many of the other practice management consultants. That's why my clients work with me for years. It's really simple. I hold them to account. I have a relationship with them that permits me to push, drive and demand actions that they would otherwise avoid.

Every two weeks, my clients and I have a phone call. My clients have to report their numbers, their results, progress on key projects, their assessment of staff performance, and their identification of problems or issues.

I act as a committed listener. And I hold them to account. I make requests (ask for commitments) for appropriate actions. "I request you speak to your front desk about her personal phone calls today and e-mail me back by 5:00 PM that you've done that." Then I check back with them to ensure they have kept their word.

You can ask any of my clients what kind of difference this makes. Having a committed listener, having someone that holds them to account, having someone who holds their feet to the fire, enables them to do what must be done. From my point of view, doing "what must be done" creates an environment of integrity, power and trust. And inside this environment, great results always get produced — and I mean always.

So my advice is to get someone who will hold you to account. Set up this structure and it will keep your head out of the sand and force you to confront reality. Within this relationship, make commitments to handle the issue or problem. Commitments are the fuel that will allow you to step into the arena with the lions. And commitments made inside a relationship of accountability are much different than commitments made to yourself on New Year's Eve. Commitments made with and inside a relationship of accountability are commitments you keep.

PASSION, PURPOSE & PROFITABILITY

I am in my 14th year of solo practice and I'd best describe my practice as uninspired. I don't have much enthusiasm going to work. Haven't had any for the last eight years. My staff seems to be there just for the money. It got so bad I stopped having staff meetings altogether. Forget morning huddles!

I thought by this time in my career I'd be making a lot more money and having far fewer problems. I tried some CE programs on business, hired a consultant once maybe seven years ago, but that didn't really do it for me. I day-dream a lot about getting out of practice, but I can't figure out what else to do. And I am so far away from fully funding my retirement, I won't be able to retire for years to come, maybe never.

I get depressed when I'm around other dentists. Some of my colleagues are far more successful than I am. I don't understand why they are and I'm not. I am in a study club with three dentists who are your clients. They seem to be really enjoying their practices and are excited all the time. I asked one of my colleagues at a recent study club why he is so successful. He said I should write you, so I'm writing you.

• ⁕ •

I don't want you to hear this as the gospel. There are 130,000 dentists in practice, so my sample size is far too small to make universal claims. But in my experience, in my perception of what is fundamental and critical to success, two elements always need to be present and these two elements seem to be missing for you. These two elements are passion and purpose.

It's very clear to me that highly successful dentists are passionate about two things. One, they are passionate about their dentistry. Two, they are passionate about their vision. What I consistently find to be true with my clients is that they are authentically passionate about their dentistry and genuinely passionate about their vision. And they are significantly more successful than those who are not.

How do I know they are passionate about their dentistry? Their passion infuses them with an unconditional commitment to clinical excellence. And where does commitment always show up? It shows up in their calendar and their checkbook.

When I look at what they read, how much CE they are doing, how many trips they take and where, who they spend their time with, what they worry about, what gets them excited, what they can't stop talking about, what their spouses complain about — well, it's obvious.

They spend a ton of money on CE. They are in programs with clinical mentors. They spend time with other dentists discussing cases. Their dentistry is never "good enough." Bottom line, they love their dentistry. They are passionate about their dentistry.

If I looked at your calendar and your checkbook, would they reflect this passion? How many days out of the office and on weekends would I see you in continuing training and education? If I looked at your e-mail, phone call records, reading materials, would they shout "*This dentist is a commitment to clinical excellence!*" If not, that's the first clue. If you're not passionate about delivering top of the line dentistry, you won't achieve success in your practice.

The second thing a successful dentist is passionate about is their vision. They have a particular view of the future. They see a future they really want to make happen. They are consumed about achieving this future. Now this future, this vision, is a particular kind of future. It is first of all a future that the dentist fully believes is possible to achieve. It is a future that isn't about him or her, but when accomplished, will make a difference for others. Again, the dentist is fully committed to making this vision happen.

Now a passionate vision leads directly to purpose. Purpose incites commitment. Commitment promotes effective action. And effective action produces results. And results produce profit. So there you have it.

I suggest you consider participating in an advanced dental training and education program focused on clinical excellence: Dawson, Pankey, Kois, Spears. Take their introductory programs and see which one is the best fit for you. Take out your checkbook and calendar and commit.

I also suggest you get yourself a practice management consultant who can coach you to generate, articulate and embody a vision. A vision that turns you on. A vision that you're willing to fight for. A vision that will infuse you with courage, commitment and drive.

If you can get passionate about your dentistry and passionate about your vision, then you will have what it takes to be successful. Without passion, without purpose, it's tough to be profitable. Complete the following form.

WHAT IS YOUR PURPOSE?

In our work, we base vision on the Collins Model:

Vision = Core Values + Beliefs + Purpose + Mission

Please consider the following and engage in this inquiry.

What is the purpose of my practice?

The difference between a good practice and a great practice is the great practice has a vibrant, powerful, purpose — a purpose that drives the practice and its people.

Complete the following Mastery formula to define your Purpose:

PURPOSE = *Ideas* *your practice is fighting for*
Values *your practice stands for*
Higher Calling *of your practice*

Purpose is about the difference you're trying to make — in your neighborhood, your community and the world. What will ensure your success is not more, better or a different of the same thing. It is having a real purpose.

The purpose of Mastery is clear. Transform dentists into highly successful businessmen and businesswomen. That's what we're fighting for. That's our higher calling. That's what our work is all about.

A purpose is your reason for existence.

What are you fighting for?

What is your purpose?

HOW TO ABSOLUTELY BEAT THE COMPETITION? QOE!

I am in my fifth year of practice in a highly competitive, high-end county of Southern California. The median house in our neighborhood is $1M. The wealth in this county naturally attracts lots of dentists. My question is, "How do I develop myself and my practice to beat the competition?"

My strategy is to become a recognized, very high-end quality dentist. Then compete on my peak competencies in restorative and cosmetic dentistry. But that's what every dentist is doing.

For the last two years, I've participated in programs with John Kois and Frank Spears and I'm about to go through Kois' entire curriculum. I would do this anyway because of who I am, but I also believe this is my strongest leverage to compete.

Do you think competing on quality is a smart strategy?

• ◦ •

First, you need to realize you can't compete and win on quality of care. Although the suppliers and pundits want you to believe the myth that quality of care is the major driver in getting people to come to you for their dentistry, it's pure fantasy. It's hogwash, hooey, nonsense. People do not select a dentist nor do they purchase their dentistry based on quality of care.

Furthermore, there is no neutral governing body that measures and reports on the quality of care delivered by dentists. There are no comparisons of one dentist's quality against any other. The fact is there are no measures, no regulatory controls, no mutually agreed upon benchmarks whatsoever, and no Six Sigma with "zero defects per hundred" measures. There are simply no available metrics to delineate quality of care. None.

The way the dental industry is set up, any dentist can claim they deliver the "very highest quality" of care. There is no way to contest this declaration, nor is there any way to validate this claim. Have you ever met a dentist who didn't argue they deliver the highest quality of care?

Fortunately, as Deming, Juran and other experts in quality management and quality improvement have demonstrated time and time again, quality can be measured (*Dr. Deming: The American Who Taught the Japanese about Quality* by Rafael Acquaro). Dentists don't measure, so how will they ever know if they are delivering quality or not? Answer: They won't.

In the dental industry, a dentist can diagnose, treatment plan and deliver any kind of care he or she wants, since care is totally unregulated, not based on evidence, and is strongly influenced by market and financial forces (*Cost Implications of Differences in Dentists' Restorative Treatment Decisions* by Daniel Shugars and James Bader, Vol. 56, No. 4, Summer of 1996, *Journal of Public Health Dentistry*).

So even though you might commit to providing the best care available, since there is no documented baseline, no quality control, no quality measures in dentistry — you simply can't compete on quality of care. If dentistry had quality measures and quality standards like car makers, it might be a whole different story. You can't do what the Japanese car makers did to compete with the American car makers since there are no markers, metrics or standards for quality.

So if you can't compete on quality of care, what can you compete on? What you can compete on is Quality of Experience or QoE. In my view, the quality of the patient's experience is the overriding determinant in the patient's perception and therefore action with a dental practice and the dentist.

Quality of Experience, as the term "experience" suggests, is multi-faceted and open-ended. What QoE does is align service quality to the QoE, which allows practices to begin to capture the full human dimension of their service performance. Two companies we worked with demonstrated that if you improve QoE, you significantly improve the bottom line. And it was dramatic.

So what is QoE? Quality of Experience is an important baseline for assessing business (practice) effectiveness vis-à-vis a number of critical business (practice) processes. Without an accurate picture of QoE for a given service, a business/practice can only speculate about its effectiveness in customer service. Here are seven key areas which are useful in measuring and managing QoE:

1. Service Availability

2. Service Responsiveness

3. Service Consistency

4. Service Appropriateness

5. Flexibility

6. Security and Compliance

7. Cost-effectiveness

It is my view that the best way to compete in dentistry is by having a clear focus on constantly improving the QoE of the patient. It's my assertion that the better the Quality of Experience, the more patients will be referred by other patients, the higher level of case acceptance and the less difficulty in collecting money.

LISTEN FOR THE MILLION DOLLARS

I was recently at a conference and attended your presentation on Staff Communication and Management. I thought it was one of the best practice management programs I have ever attended. I wish I'd learned more about communication years ago when I started my practice.

I was one of the dentists who came up to you after your presentation. I asked you about what you thought the major difference between dentists who do 6-figures and those that did 7-figures. You said something I didn't clearly understand, but there were a number of other dentists waiting to ask you questions, so I left without asking more.

You said that the difference between a dentist who runs a $750K practice and one that has a $1.2 million practice is "how they listened." Not sure what you meant by that. Can you explain?

• ◦ •

A large percentage of my coaching clients have 7-figure practices. I'm not sure why I ended up being their consultant of choice. Maybe I'm just lucky, or maybe I have models, methods and perspectives that fit well for this particular group of dentist-business-owners. Maybe I have an in-depth grasp of their issues and concerns. Maybe I understand they each have unique and individual expressions that are distinctive and that need to be enhanced. Maybe I'm smart enough to realize that one size doesn't fit all and there is no single prescribed recipe for success. Maybe developing the person as a leader, manager and owner, trusting they know what's best for them and their practice is the way to go. Well, at least a few dentists think so.

Anytime I am asked questions like yours, I always need to qualify my assertions. I always feel I need to say that my experience is limited to those dentists I work with so my observations are not "the truth." My perspective is formed from what I've seen over and over again in my particular clients' million-plus dollar practices, and from helping lots of dentists achieve the million dollar mark over the last decade.

As I see it, all dentists wear many difference hats and play many different roles in service to their practice. One hat says manager. One says owner. One says marketer. Another hat says leader. Most of the time, of course, they wear a hat called clinician. In this regard, nearly all dentists wear the same hats and are assigned the same roles. But the 7-figure dentists seems to play the leadership and manager roles differently than the 6-figure dentist.

Both the 6-figure and 7-figure dentists have staff. Both surround themselves with people who have specific job duties to perform, certain accountabilities to fulfill. But the 6-figure dentist falls into the trap of thinking that their responsibility is to be the person who makes all the decisions, the one who must have all the answers. The "answer-man" blindly believing he or she must be the final arbiter of all conflicts, decisions and dilemmas. This places them in a very lonely and isolated position where information becomes unreliable and useful input is stifled.

Running their practice as the "answer-man" is clearly a product of their dental education and training, a culture where they were taught they are the ones. During their time in dental school, they rarely if ever work as team to deliver a result. Sure they have an assistant from time to time, but it is only to assist the young dentist in doing their individual work on a patient. It isn't much of a leap for the dentist to assume that because he or she is solely responsible for all the clinical decisions, that he or she is fully responsible for all the business decisions as well.

Even though both the 6-figure and 7-figure dentists go about hiring good people, it's the 6-figure dentists who can't shake this dental upbringing, "It is always up to me." This results in the 6-figure dentists failing to listen to people around them. Somehow 7-figure dentists break the bonds of their training and listen to those around them.

Now when staff makes suggestions about improving operations or enhancing patient service, the 6-figure dentist takes little notice of their recommendations. They use their position of power to drown out real discussion. Frustrated, staff soon grasps the implicit message that they are neither heard nor valued, so they shut down and become resigned or they leave.

By the way, when you look at turnover rates, you'll see a much higher frequency, at least in my experience, with 6-figure practices than 7-figure practices. The pay scales are basically the same in both. So it might well be the simple fact that listening to your staff decreases turnover.

The 7-figure dentist understands his or her role is to bring out answers in others. They do this by seeking contributions, challenges and collaboration from their staff. They use their position of power not to dominate but rather to drive the decision-making process. The more collaborative, less territorial and less political the process is, the less isolated the dentist-leader and the greater likelihood whatever is decided will be carried out.

At a typical staff meeting with a 7-figure dentist, you notice he or she doesn't blame or fault others, but holds the team accountable for finding a solution. He or she conveys the message they are all there to help each other to find the answer. It's not his or her job to provide the answers, but rather to help find the best solutions. This approach stimulates collaboration and the people around him contribute. Contribution leads to ownership. So when a solution is reached, everyone owns it.

So what I said before is essentially this: The difference between a 6- and 7-figure dentist is the 7-figure dentist knows how to listen.

CONCRETENESS

I set monthly goals in production and new patients but never make them. Maybe I'm doing something wrong. How do you set goals so they motivate the staff and yourself to achieve the goals?

• • •

It's no wonder you are not making your goals. You are defining your goals in such a way that your staff doesn't know what to focus on and, therefore, what actions to take.

"Our goal for the month is 22 new patients."

What is the staff supposed to do about that?

It might be a lot better to set more specific daily goals — goals that they can do. Such as, "I request you speak to two people a day about being a new patient in our office." They can't do much about 22 new patients a month but they can do something about handing out two cards a day.

Most dentists set goals that have no power. They set goals that are so ambiguous, so undefined, so generalized, that the goals fail to encourage action and promote alignment. Everyone knew what the goals were when John Kennedy declared that we put a man on the moon by the end of the decade. No ambiguity there. No room for too much individual interpretation. No misunderstanding. Not much to misunderstand about "man," "moon," or "end of the decade."

The more concrete your goals, the more attainable they are. The more generalized your goals the more open to interpretation, or misinterpretation. The more interpretation generated the less coordinated action. The more generalized your goals the further out of reach they seem to be. The more generalized your goals the more unrealistic, unmanageable and unattainable they appear to the staff.

"Specificity to goals adds power."

Specificity adds clarity. Specificity removes interpretation. Specificity enhances commitment. And specificity generates alignment. When everyone is crystal clear on the goal, when there is no wiggle-room for interpretation of the goal, alignment is much more easily achieved. Alignment delivers a "we" rather than a bunch of "I's." And "we" is a lot more powerful, effective and produces far better results than "I."

You want to set goals in a way that people can commit to them. You want to set goals that you and your staff hold as really possible to achieve. If you and your staff don't hold the goals as truly possible, you and your staff won't make authentic commitments. You need possibility in the background to have commitments in the foreground. The more concrete, specific and tangible your goals, the more powerful and effective your promises and requests are going to be.

So besides making your goals concrete, you need to add another piece to setting goals. This is critical and fundamental to achieving the goals. It requires leadership. You need to get people to see that making the defined goals is possible. If they feel that the goal is pie in the sky or unattainable, they will not commit to making it happen. No commitment, little effective action.

And for you to generate possibility,

"You yourself must hold the goal as possible to achieve."

If not, if it's just a wish or a hope, and chances are slim it will happen. Also, goals by themselves don't motivate staff. You need to demonstrate how they will forward the mission and make the vision real. Staff doesn't care about how many new patients you generate. They're going to get paid anyway. But they do care if treating more new patients makes a difference to the health and well being of a family.

If the goal is concrete and you generate possibility, then what should follow are authentic commitments to accomplish the goal. Commitment leads to effective action. Effective action delivers results. "I'm going to lose weight" is much weaker than "I promise to lose 12 pounds over the next four months. I now weight 172 and I will weight 160 by the target date. I promise to take the following actions each week. I will begin this tomorrow."

The Heath brothers in their book *Made to Stick* give this example. "When Boeing prepared to launch the design of the 727 passenger plane in the 1960s, its managers set a goal that was deliberately concrete: *The 727 must seat 131 passengers, fly nonstop from Miami to New York City, and land on Runway 4-22* at La Guardia (They chose Runway 4-22 because of its length — less than mile, which until this time was too short for any existing passenger jet). With a goal this concrete, Boeing coordinated the actions of thousands of experts. Imagine how much harder it would have been to have built a 727 whose goal was to be "the best passenger plane in the world."

My recommendation is that you break down your goals into very tangible, measurable components. And also bring in leadership to make achieving this goal appear as possible. Finally you need to bring in management and generate and manage commitments in the form of promises and requests. I suggest you do these three things and you will start to make your goals consistently.

IN BUSINESS AND IN LIFE, IT'S ALL ABOUT RELATIONSHIPS

I have been in practice for 14 years and I just can't seem to get over the hump. I've tried just about everything to move the practice beyond middle-of-the-road. By middle-of-the-road I mean I can't produce any more than $500K or generate more than 8-10 new patients a month. My classmates from dental school are doing $250-$500 K more than I am.

I've worked with two nationally known consultants, one six years ago and one two years ago. They came to my office and worked with the staff and myself. We had phone calls and e-mails as well. One consultant cost me $17,400 and the other was close to $30,000. That doesn't include the travel we did to attend their programs they provided for their clients. They gave us lots of materials, manuals, CDs, etc.

I tried hard to follow their recommendations, recipes and tips. I used their methods and materials, you know — the whole nine yards. But given my production, collection and new patients, I still can't get the practice to operate beyond $525,000 per year.

Maybe I'm doing something wrong. What is the right formula to generating revenues over $850,000?

• ◦ •

You know acid will turn blue litmus paper to red. You know that lengthening one side of a right triangle will have a predictable effect on the length of the hypotenuse. Science and math are the way you think, the way you were trained. So of course you would think that by applying the *right formula,* you'll produce a successful practice.

If only business operated like math or organic chemistry, where well-established principles and rules determined the outcome. Then, you'd have it all figured out. You'd know exactly how to run your practice as a successful business. But as you are discovering, it just doesn't work that way.

Dentists are suckers for charts, graphs, metrics and maps that imply the formula for business success:

A + B = $

And of course, these formulas are spoken by consultants, each pitching their formula as the answer. This motivates dentists to attend their lectures, off-sites and training programs and spend tons of money on their manuals, CDs and books, because they know that dentists are urgently searching for the holy grail of formulas.

Business success is based on people — your staff and your patients. People are unpredictable, chaotic, erratic and random. Science and mathematics applied here won't work. There are no formulas or recipes that hold true in the domain of people, and the business of dental practice is about people. So what then determines practice success?

A successful practice has successful relationships with people — and that's key. And to have successful relationships, you need to do two things: 1) Make people feel important and 2) create trust.

The first step is to make your patients and your staff members feel important. My cousin, Steven, is salesperson at Barney's in New York. He encloses a note with every package he sends to his customers. He makes his customers feel important.

Jonathan is a senior partner in a venture capital firm I worked with in Silicon Valley. He calls the CEOs of the companies he's invested in every Monday morning. He doesn't have an agenda; he just let's them know he is there to help. Jon's clients are reminded that they are important. Make your patients feel important and make your staff feel important.

At the same time, you need to generate TRUST with your patients and your staff. Trust is the key to any successful relationship. But what is trust? Trust is a feeling that we can depend on the other person. But what produces trust?

In any close relationship with a dysfunctional person, you eventually realize it isn't the dysfunctional person's behavior that damages the relationship, but their utter inconsistency, their unpredictability. You cannot depend on the person to be or do one thing or another. It causes you to pull away.

In a successful relationship, each party can predict the other's behavior. Successful dental practices are predictable. So to build trust, build consistency in everything you do.

Another element that is fundamental to trust is INTEGRITY. People value integrity. We realize integrity has a heroic quality since it often requires courage. But in a service business patients value integrity in that the practice keeps its promises, which makes at least part of their lives more predictable. A practice's integrity makes patients' lives more convenient and more comfortable by being predictable. So to build trust, give your word and do everything you can to keep it.

To generate powerful and successful relationships, both with patients and with staff, they need to know you will act predictably, act and speak with integrity and do nothing to harm them — ever. You must generate relationships of trust and have people feel important. Do that and your practice will take off!

THE LONE RANGER RIDES AGAIN

I am sick and tired of my colleagues telling me to contact you. I have always done it on my own. I use common sense to run my business and I've been moderately successful without any consulting, coaching or advice.

Sure, some of my colleagues have more successful practices, but it looks like they are addicted to hiring consultants and coaches like you. What a waste of time and money.

Give me one good reason why I need someone like you.

• ∘ •

First, ask yourself would you rather be right or happy? My bet right now is you'd rather be right.

You can get to be right and have a moderately successful practice, or you could be wrong and risk having a tremendously successful practice. It's your choice.

You're like a lot of dentists, thinking you should be able to do it on your own. Well, in my view, this thinking is totally ego-driven and fueled by false pride. What if this perspective was stopping you from being outrageously successful? Would it be worth it to change your position?

First of all, you are coming from a position that you've got all you need to succeed, rather than focusing on results. You're out to prove you have what it takes, rather than looking for ways to enhance your business success. Well, I guess it comes down to a matter of priorities — you looking successful or the practice being successful. Well, what's your preference?

What are you afraid of? Do you think you'll look weak or foolish to your fellow dentists, family or community? Have you been arguing, "Who needs a consultant, who needs a coach? Because if you can't do it yourself, you must be a loser?"

There's a universal principle, "Whatever you focus on expands." Whatever you direct your intention and attention to expands. In your case, your eyes aren't on results, they're on "You." When you are more committed to success than being right or looking good, then you don't care how your success happens or with how many people you have to share your success.

From my point of view, setting your ego and identity aside and seeking help is a sign of strength, not weakness. It demonstrates you're committed to success, not committed to looking good to others. If you are only committed to making a good living, rather than building a very successful business, then that's all your practice will ever provide for you. And you'll get to be right.

But ask yourself if that's why you went into private practice? Wasn't there something beyond giving yourself a good job? Didn't you go into practice to have a great business?

My experience shows that people who are truly committed to success always get help. They don't let their ego, their identity or their pride get in the way. They connect with people who will help them and are not afraid of doing it.

Success isn't a mystery. Success leaves clues. Once you stop trying to prove that you can do it alone, drop your ego and look for help, then magically people appear who will teach you what they know about success.

So stop hiding behind doing it "your way," doing it on "your own," sink or swim, hoping someday it will all work out. Stop fighting the good fight, staying up all those late nights, not taking vacations, feeling a kind of loneliness. It isn't a matter of pride or self-esteem to find the answer on your own. It isn't a matter of using common sense to make the business work. Successful people get lots of help because success is a result of a group not an individual.

Even the Lone Ranger had Tonto!

CONTEXT OF LEADERSHIP

The action of LEADERSHIP is speaking. Leaders speak of a future in the present. They do not speak of a future that is pie-in-the-sky or a future that is simply an extension of the past. Leaders speak for a future, a future that is not about them, but about something that will make a lasting difference.

LEADERS speak in such a way that they engage people emotionally so they can be part of making that future happen. Leaders articulate the future in a way people can envision themselves being a part of that future and helping it come to pass.

LEADERS are unconditionally committed to making their vision of the future happen. By being committed, by speaking of a future so others can see it and feel it, they get people moving in the same direction. Also, by speaking of the future, leaders offload their own agendas and lessen their need to be right, to dominate and to have everything go their way. They seek the best way, not the "right" way. They create a condition of commitment, alignment and workability.

RELOCATE TO GREATNESS

I have a good practice. We are above average in new patients and production in our area. But being good is not being great. How do I create a great practice?

. . .

You have a very common problem, a problem that affects many dentists. There are many good practices. In fact, most dental practices are "good" practices. Moving your practice to "great," however, begins with leadership.

Good is the enemy of great. Good makes you complacent. Good makes you comfortable. Good diminishes your willingness to take risks. Good forces you to play it safe. You will never move your practice to great by reducing risk. So, first you have to be willing to risk good. But most dentists are too risk-averse to make that leap. The first question you have to answer for yourself is this: Is "good enough" good enough? If it is, you will never have a truly great practice.

In my work with dental practices over the past two decades, I have discovered something truly unexpected about dentists who have turned good practices into great practices. Even I can be surprised! I thought that great practices would have charismatic leaders. But what I have learned is dentists with great practices are not usually high-profile types with huge egos.

I have found that leaders of great practices are much more humble, reserved, quiet and even self-effacing. But what each of them has is an enormous intention to be the very best. These dentists are much more focused on having a great practice than on getting their picture on the cover of *Dental Economics*. They aren't concerned about being a star on the lecture circuit as much as they are about having a five-star practice.

Another universal characteristic of dentists with great practices is they have the right people on their staffs. They have the right people on their teams and they aren't afraid to get the wrong people off. And they make sure the right people are in the right positions.

Most dentists are wimps when it comes to hiring and firing. But the leaders of great practices hold firm that the right team is far more important than their fear of firing someone. They assemble the right team and they're willing to fire people to keep it together.

The leaders of great practices also have an authentic vision. A future they are wholeheartedly committed to achieving. A future beyond soundly beating the local competition in new patients or revenues. A future beyond their personal income. A future that is not identity-based. A future that makes a difference to the patients their practices serve. These dentists envision a future that challenges their practices every day to perform at the highest level possible.

Dentists in great practices declare their vision in a way that others can understand clearly. They speak in such a way that others are inspired and personally committed to making the vision real. By speaking in this way, these dentists align their staffs and improve the way people work together.

Finally, I've found these leaders place tremendous demands on themselves and have high expectations for themselves and their teams to perform at the highest level. They hold integrity as the most sacred value and demand that people honor their word as themselves.

In fact, in my view, what ultimately moves a practice to "great" is integrity — the ability to give your word and keep it. That is what leads to great performance. When who you are is an unconditional commitment to operate as *your* word, when you hold others fully accountable for *their* word, then you have the power to create a great practice.

BORED, APATHETIC & INDIFFERENT

NO MYSTERY WHY
YOUR STAFF LEAVES

I have a very high turnover of staff. Ten people over the last eight years. Not sure why they up and leave. One thing I keep on seeing, no matter who I have on staff, is that staff members always looks so disinterested at our meetings and huddles.

I can't get them enthusiastic about their jobs or the practice. I've tried everything — from CE programs, in-house consultants, CDs — you name it, I've spent money on it.

We went to the ADA and came to your presentation on Staff Communication and Management. We all left inspired. We all left turned on. But within weeks, it was back to the same-old, same-old.

How can I fix my staff and then keep them inspired?

. . .

To inspire your staff, you need to be inspiring. It all begins and ends with you. And for you to be inspiring, you need to be inspired yourself. You can't "give it" unless you "got it." So you need to start with yourself first.

If you're like many dentists, what's at the bottom of your lack of inspiration is your overriding focus on making a good living. You unconsciously hold your practice as a way to give yourself a good job, not to build a great business. This is the fatal flaw.

You consider your practice a kind of comfort blanket which will keep you safe, happy and financially secure. You have the practice *for* and *about you.* You unconsciously have the practice be for you, so the practice can take care of you. And you wonder why the staff is not inspired. How can they be when the practice is about you? What's inspiring about that?

I know the usual rhetoric about great patient care and doing the best for patients and quality care. But walk and talk are very different.

There is nothing the practice is going for. There is nothing the practice is up to. There is nothing the practice wants to accomplish besides its own survival — so it can pay the bills and pay you.

In order to be inspirational, stirring, rousing, you need to access that part of you and then let it be expressed. Staff is inspired by working in a practice that takes risks to make something special happen. Staff is inspired by a dentist who puts his or her life on the line to make a difference for others. And, as I said above, and this is conjecture, most likely you're risk adverse and the practice isn't up to making a real and lasting difference.

Where do you begin? Well, you begin by generating and committing to a future that's possible. By a future that's possible I mean something other than a future that is a dream or just more of the same. A future that is possible is not solely about you. By possible I mean likely, probable, promising, viable, achievable. A future that you see will make a difference. A future that has the clear and present possibility of impacting peoples' lives and health. A future that you would be willing to take big risks to make happen.

If you embrace a future that's possible, you will feel an emotional charge, a kind of energy boost. Then you know you are opening the gate to inspiration. You feel creative. You feel an urge to take action. You feel courageous. You feel stimulated to make something happen. That's inspired.

When you take a look at successful dentists who inspire their staff, you see practices that are up to big things. Dentists who have the guts to put themselves and their practice at-stake to make it happen. It isn't about the revenues. It isn't about the dentist's personal income or retirement. It is about creating a practice that will impact their community in such a way that peoples' lives and health are altered.

My first piece of coaching is to read the following books in this order:

The Secret by Blanchard
9 Lies That Hold Your Business Back by Chandler
The Art of Possibility by Zander
The Last Word on Power by Goss

Then, create a future for your practice that puts you at risk and go for it. Now that's inspiring.

THE RULES OF LEADERSHIP

I have a colleague who is in the Mastery program. Her practice has definitely been impacted within a very short period of time. Her staff is performing better, she has more patients, she is making more money and she is happier. When I ask her why, she tells me she is a much better "leader." What's going on? Can you define what a leader is?

. . .

Here are my 22 Rules of Leadership. If you apply them, if you continuously check yourself against them and if you deliver on them, you will be a powerful leader in your practice. Unfortunately, they are necessarily a bit "jargon-y," so you will need to have your colleague help you understand what is meant by each rule. But she is becoming a Master and she will be happy to assist you in your quest.

1. What you know about leadership isn't leadership.

2. Leadership is a verb.

3. Leadership is an existential act of real courage. You can't work your way up to it.

4. Leaders call people to be bigger than they see themselves to be.

5. Leaders make unreasonable requests.

6. Leaders make bold promises.

7. Leadership is going from nothing to inventing an intention, then bringing that intention to reality as accomplishment.

8. Leadership makes vision something that can be fulfilled, and not just a good idea.

9. Leaders know a vision is not an ideal, because it's not something you "have."

10. Leaders direct what is already there, that wants to happen, but that wasn't going to happen without intervention.

11. Leaders are intentional. Leaders speak through declaration. They speak "what shall be."

12. Leaders know that life doesn't care.

13. Leaders aren't better at doing it; they are better at starting and then sorting it out as it unfolds.

14. Leadership is not neutral. Leaders are unrelentingly one-way about it.

15. Leaders create a background of honor to one's word. They don't handle people's "cases."

16. Leaders know they will have to continuously deal with peoples' resignation. Their job is to transform it.

17. Leaders deal with people's "stories" by taking the payoff out of it.

18. Leadership is not a memory-based phenomenon; it is created in the moment — moment by moment.

19. Leaders create by acknowledging.

20. Leaders elicit peoples' participation and contribution, not their opinions or complaints.

21. Leadership is never given; it is always taken.

22. Leaders don't know any more than you do.

My coaching to you is to go be a leader this week and see what it gives you.

LEADING VS. MANAGING

In the last seven years, I have spent a total of $76,000 on practice management consulting and practice management programs. I now have the "best of breed" of management systems — practice management software, manuals, scripts, flow charts, budgets, targets, brand, logo, structured staff meetings, Website and the rest. Still, my staff isn't performing nearly as well as I know it could in terms of getting the job done, being a team and marketing the practice better.

I know I am managing better, yet I am not getting the staff performance I expect.

What's going on?

• ○ •

Your problem is lack of leadership, not lack of management. You have collapsed "management" with "leadership." Like most dentists, you are over-managing and under-leading.

Here's the source of your problem: You think that management and leadership are the same thing. That's why you keep on investing more into management, yet leadership is nowhere to be found. You need to understand that leadership is different from management.

Leadership isn't mystical or mysterious. It is not the province of a chosen few. Nor is leadership necessarily better than management. They are just different.

Leadership and management are complementary systems of action. Each has its own function and characteristic activities and both are necessary for practice success. Your management is fine. It's leadership that's missing.

Why do dentists focus so much on management and so little on leadership? The reason is dentists are extremely risk-averse. That aversion to risk is one of the primary drivers of dentists' choosing their profession. With that relationship to risk, dentists believe that the more management they create the less risk they'll have to endure.

Complexity not handled turns into chaos. Chaos always increases risk. The greater the complexity, the greater the risk. The more successful a dental practice becomes, the more complex it becomes as well. Management is about coping with complexity. Dentists try to reduce risk by putting all of their attention and effort into managing complexity. They use management to bring order and consistency to the key dimensions of the practice so they can have control and, therefore, reduce chaos and handle the risk. All that is fine, but it's got nothing to do with leadership. Management is coping with complexity. Leadership is coping with change.

Management does its thing by organization and staffing. Management develops an organizational structure and a set of jobs to achieve the results. Management gets it done by delegating responsibilities to qualified individuals, communicating what needs to get done, devising systems to monitor implementation. None of that is the job of leadership.

What leadership does is align people by communicating the direction of the practice set by the vision. Leadership generates commitment toward achieving that vision.

Management ensures the results by controlling and problem-solving — monitoring results with reports, meetings and various measurements. When results aren't being produced, management addresses the problems.

Leadership, on the other hand, focuses on the vision. To achieve the vision, leadership motivates and inspires people. Leaders invoke inspiration using values and emotions. The function of leadership is to produce change. Setting the direction of that change is Job One for a leader. Setting the direction is not the same as planning. Planning is a management process, deductive in nature. Setting a direction is a leadership process and is inductive in nature.

My feeling is you are not being a leader in your practice. You are not generating a true and powerful vision for your practice — one that pulses though the practice and excites, aligns and empowers your staff. Don't stop managing, but do start leading!

YOU CAN'T "DO" LEADERSHIP

I have been trying hard to be a leader in my practice ever since I started seven years ago. I'm just not making it happen. I read books, go to lectures, listen to tapes. Nothing seems to really help.

When I lead staff meetings or morning huddles, I know the staff doesn't get excited. I can't inspire them to go for it. In fact, most of the time, they just look plain uninterested. Worse, this also happens with some of my patients.

How do I become a strong leader? What should I do?

• ※ •

I'm sorry to tell you, you have it all wrong. There is nothing to "do" to become a leader. You can't become a leader by "doing." Being and doing are not the same. Being and doing are very much different from one another. Doing is action. Being is where the action is coming from. Being precedes doing.

So the only way to become a leader is by altering who you are being as a leader. Being can't be altered by doing. It doesn't work that way. I've been training and developing dentists as leaders for many years and in my experience, shifting a dentist's way of being consistently develops them as effective leaders.

I know. The next question is how do you change someone's being? Since it isn't about doing something, then what? How do you change someone's way of being?

First, you have to realize that leaders come in all shapes and sizes. There are no must-have characteristics. You've got everything it takes to be a leader. You don't need to be charismatic, forceful or upbeat. What I've found over the years are strong leaders possess nine core elements that allow them be effective leaders.

These nine elements are about who they are being — not what they do. If you embody these nine elements with rigor, discipline and high intention, you will become an effective leader.

1) *Maintain Absolute Integrity*

   This is fundamental and critical. You must do whatever you can to honor yourself as your word. No compromises. No excuses. No reasons. There is no 90 percent. You've got to be 100 percent. *Be your word.*

2) *Know Your Stuff and If You Don't Know, Say So*

   It's simple. You cannot exaggerate, make stuff up, embellish or try to gain sympathy by making your staff feel sorry for you. Leadership is not about being liked. It's not about being well thought of. And it certainly isn't about looking good. If you don't know the answer, say so and then find out. *Be truthful, candid and straightforward.*

3) *Be Responsible*

   You must, at all times, hold yourself responsible. You are always the bottom line. To be responsible you must stand for "I am cause in the matter." You can't blame, shame, apply guilt or fault to others or to circumstances because that is the antithesis of responsibility. *Be responsible.*

4) *Declare Your Vision*

   Leaders bring a future to the present now. Their speech is declarative in nature. A declaration is the most powerful of all the speech acts. A declaration is beyond a promise. A declaration is beyond a request. A declaration is a statement where you and what you speak are one. A leader declares a future so that others see it as possible and are willing to commit to achieving it, and this can only be accomplished through an authentic declaration. *Be your vision in speaking and action.*

5) *Show Unconditional Commitment*

   Most people make commitments that are conditional. "I'll do it if that happens. I'll produce the result if this happens. I'll generate more new patients if such and such happens." A leader knows in business and in life you either have your reasons or your results. As a leader you deliver no matter the conditions. *Be committed no matter what.*

6) *Produce Results*
Napoleon Hill discovered within every disadvantage or obstacle there is an equally powerful opportunity. Successful leaders look for and find these opportunities. Leaders do what they need to do, without sacrificing their core values, and produce the result. *Be unyielding about producing results.*

7) *Take Care of Your People*
Leaders authentically care about their staff. They care about them as people, not just employees. They care about their futures, families, health and well being. They care about them being the best they can be — professionally and personally. *Be in service to your staff.*

8) *Put Duty Before Self*
Leaders place duty to their patients, duty to their practice and duty to their staff ahead of themselves. Leaders have a silent credo — duty, honor, quality and service — which they hold as sacred.

9) *Stand Out in Front*
Leaders stand in front of their staff. They take the heat. They don't abdicate their responsibilities. They don't offload criticism. They are brave by always stepping into the issues or problems first. They take the heat before letting it be caught by others. *Be willing to always stay out in front.*

Armed with this information, now the question is can you be these elements in action. Can you embody them, live them and honor them. Give it your best effort for two weeks and see what that gives you. If you embrace and practice these nine core elements, if you "be" these elements, you will be a very powerful leader.

LOOK AT THE DOER, NOT THE DEED!

I have been in practice 16 years. A number of my colleagues who started their practices at the same time are now doing much better financially. What are they doing that I'm not doing?

I feel like there is something wrong with me because I can't produce the kind of numbers and results they do. I work very hard, read the practice management literature, attend programs, belong to study clubs and have had two practice management consultants over the last six years. There was improvement, but it did not bring the production and new patient levels I wanted.

What are other dentists doing that I am not doing that makes them so successful?

•　○　•

Like most dentists, you seek answers in the wrong place. You fervently believe the answers lie in the domain of the deed. "Do" the right thing, "take" the right steps and you will be successful. That is a myth. Those selling their solutions are fooling you. You are being duped, conned, manipulated and hoodwinked. Why? Because what you "do" is not the key to success.

The answers you seek live in the domain of the "doer," not the deed. So don't spend your time trying to learn what to "do," spend your time learning who you need to "be."

Start looking at the "doer" not the "deed."

Let me give you the bottom line here. What I have found is highly successful dentist-practice owners are committed to mastering eight tasks.

1. They are committed to addressing "what needs to be done."
2. They are committed to doing "what is right for the practice."
3. They develop action plans.
4. They are responsible for their decisions.

5.   They take responsibility for communicating.
6.   They are focused on opportunities rather than problems.
7.   They run productive meetings.
8.   They think and act "we" rather than "I."

Highly successful dentists are always, and I mean always, asking themselves the first two questions. "What needs to be done?" and "What is right for the practice?" I'll bet the ranch you don't ask yourself those questions. The questions you probably ask yourself are "What do I want to do?" and "What do I want?"

Asking those questions and seeking answers to them results in ineffectual actions. Highly successful practice owners know it isn't about them, it is about the practice. Asking, "What will make me happy or rich or decrease my stress?" is your first mistake. Ask yourself instead, "What needs to be done now to make my practice successful?"

When you ask the first two questions — "What needs to be done?" and "What is right for the practice?" — you immediately see things you need to do that you are not doing and, in fact, are most likely avoiding doing. If you address those questions directly, you will immediately see what is stopping your practice from being successful. Firing a staff individual. Demanding performance from your team. Getting your charts done. Making sure your cases are returned from the lab on time. Asking patients for referrals. Get the picture?

Highly successful dentists are invariably engaged in the issues the first two questions bring up, and their answers lead them to doing the right things to make their practices successful. Then they go about mastering the remaining six tasks so they can effectively implement the answers they come up with when asking the first two questions.

Start with the first two questions, then master numbers 3 through 8, and you'll be on your way!

WHAT LEADERS DO

I am fairly new in practice and I want to be a strong leader. I am not sure where to begin or what I should be doing. Give me some of that sage advice on becoming an effective leader.

• ◦ •

First, you must understand that leadership is a verb, not a noun. That is critical to recognize. Leadership shows up in action, not as a set of characteristics or qualities. "Charismatic," "unwavering," "steadfast," "determined" and "passionate" are characteristics or qualities people ascribe to leaders. But that is not "leadership." Leadership is an action that moves others to commit and act themselves.

So, what do leaders take action on? In my view of leadership, there are five areas on which leaders continuously act.

THE FUTURE

Leaders speak about the future, and they constantly work on making it happen. They see the future. They have a vision of what the future will look like, how it will unfold and the difference it will make. Their daily actions and interactions are about making that future happen. Leaders are passionate about making the future real in the world.

So, your first step as a leader is creating a compelling vision for your practice. A vision that will consume you. A vision that you are passionate about, that you ardently want to make happen. Without an authentic vision, you'll never be a leader.

STAFF DEVELOPMENT

Leaders continuously take steps to develop themselves and their staffs — and that particular aspect is what is commonly weak or missing in many dentists' leadership. What is meant by development is not just improving your own and other peoples' abilities and skills related to getting the job done — although that is part of it. Development is also enabling people to better understand themselves so they can be better and more able human beings.

Most dentists are reluctant to spend their time and money on self-development or staff development. If you examine the programs, courses and seminars the majority of dentists attend, few, if any, will be focused on self-discovery, self-understanding or self-awareness. Because there is no demand for those programs, few, if any, are offered.

The majority of dentists give little credence to the power of self-actualization. They overlook this universal principle: "The observed and the observer are one." They fail to realize that to make changes in their practices, they must first change themselves. There are numerous programs and teachers in self-development. My recommendation is to find one. And focus on finding out who you are and why you think and act the way you do. You can't change anything until you change yourself.

GETTING BETTER AND BETTER

Leaders are constantly looking for new and better ways to make the future happen. They are never satisfied with their organizations' current velocity or growth in making things happen. They are continuously reinventing their business processes, upgrading their technologies and working on improving their own and their staffs' performance. Leaders are always seeking a better way to get it done.

A time-tested method for improving performance is coaching. In many cases, successful business leaders use coaches. They realize that coaches push them beyond their own self-imagined constraints, resulting in their performing at a much higher level. Like committed professional athletes, leaders know coaches directly enhance performance. Great leaders know this: "You alone must do it, but you can't do it alone."

RESULTS AND RELATIONSHIPS

Successful leaders value two things — results and relationships. They realize they must produce the bottom-line and top-line results, but they also realize that in business as well as in life, it's all about relationships.

In the area of results, dentists rank high. Most dentists are tuned in to the bottom-line results. They measure. They target. They set goals. They know which activities are required to produce results, and they lead and manage with an intention to promote actions that will lead to those results.

Where most dentists are blind is in the area of relationships. They often perceive staff as "hired helpers," people who should do their jobs so the results get produced. They spend zero time trying to develop relationships of trust, affinity and commitment with their staffs. How do I know that? I look at where they spend their time and money and more than likely it has nothing to do with building great relations with their staffs. But if you don't care about them, if you don't support them in their lives, if you're not concerned about your staff, they won't care about their jobs — or about you. Great leaders invest their time and energy in people. You can be either a serving leader or a self-serving leader.

WALKING THE TALK

Leaders, in order to lead others, must be trusted. All genuine leadership is built on trust. How leaders generate trust is by totally embodying their core values. Leaders operate in a manner consistent with the values they profess. They "walk the talk," they don't "stumble the mumble."

The major problem is most dentists practice solo. They have no one but themselves to hold them accountable for sticking to their values, operating in a manner consistent with their principles and rigorously honoring themselves as their word. But then again, that might be why dentists prefer to practice solo. Most businesses have built into their organizational structures individuals to report to — individuals who hold people accountable for their words and actions. Those individuals and their relationships include the CEO and the Board of Directors, the Vice President of Marketing and the CEO and the Board and the stockholders. Being accountable to another is simply not present in most dental practices.

Whether you use an advisor, consultant, colleague or veteran staff person, find someone you trust and empower that person to hold you accountable. Someone who won't let you off the hook, who demands you keep your word. That is what I do for my clients and it makes the biggest difference.

If you attend to those five areas every day, if you have an authentic commitment to produce and expand them every day, if you are willing to have them as your focus, you'll be a very powerful leader.

WHAT'S MISSING IS LEADERSHIP

I have a good friend who is in your Mastery program and producing great results. I am using another consultant and we are doing very similar activities. However, I don't seem to be getting nearly the same level of enthusiasm and outcomes from my staff that Greg is getting from his.

I have spent a good deal of time developing a great vision, a mission and solid core values. I have been to your Website and seen what Mastery folks have done and my vision is as good as any of theirs. But my friend has his staff really inspired and performing within the vision and acting much more like a team.

Why?

• • •

That's a great question. Although both of you have vibrant visions, missions and authentic core values, you are not getting the job done as a leader and your friend is. What is missing is *leadership*.

Yes, having a vision is critical to leadership. Being on a mission is fundamental to leadership. Having clear and solid core values and an inspiring purpose are essential to leadership. But leadership is really a verb, not a noun. And you are underperforming as a leader. More than likely, you are not effectively interacting with your staff.

To change people's behavior, you need to directly impact their feelings. The heart of change is in the emotions. You need to produce a "see-feel-change" state more than an "analysis-think-change" state. The distinctions between seeing and analyzing and between feeling and thinking are critical.

Not only do you need to present the reasons, information and images of where you are going and why, you need to touch your staff at the emotional level as well.

You are now wondering, "How do I impact my staff at the emotional level?"

The answer is simple. *Urgency.* You need to be truly urgent about the vision being realized. You need to be urgent about you and the staff adhering to your core values as if they are sacred. You need to be urgent that the purpose of the practice be realized. You need to be urgent that the mission be accomplished. Urgent! When you become urgent, you will start to get some real change. But it starts with you and the urgency you bring to the game. "Let's go! We need to move forward!"

Most dentists are afraid to be urgent. Many dentists are complacent about the way the practice and staff are performing. Often they are immobilized, self-protective, sort of hiding in the closet, fearful of making changes. They often have staff members who have the attitude that "you can't make me do it." Add to that the fact that most dentists are conflict-averse and afraid to confront their staffs and you can understand why not much change ever happens.

My question to you is this: "Are you willing to be urgent? I mean really, authentically, sincerely urgent about making your vision real?"

Only when you are willing to take a risk will the staff know you are not kidding. Who is running the practice, you or the staff? What is leading the practice, your vision or your fears?

Your relationship to the accomplishment of the vision determines the condition in which the staff relates to that vision. My grandmother had a wonderful twist on a popular expression: "A fish stinks from the head." You are that head. If you are urgent about fulfilling your vision, about being on purpose, about achieving the mission, so will your staff.

I'VE LOST MY PASSION

I have written to you several times about becoming burned out. I am a 51-year-old general practitioner in Washington State. I have a good practice and make good money. My core staff people have been with me for a while and we get along well. I stay current through CE programs and study clubs. From the outside, it looks great. But inside I am losing my passion, my desire and my drive. I can't imagine doing this for another 15 to 20 years, but I need the income.

You've responded to my concerns in the past by saying that I've lost the sense and experience of "possibility" and that I am now resigned to that state of affairs. You say that I've lost my vision because possibility is the core of vision and without the one, there is none of the other. You've asked that I develop a compelling and vibrant future, one that I can commit to, and that I then go about making it happen. You've told me to get off my duff and really go for it and see what happens.

So I asked in the past, "How do I do that?"

You responded, "Begin by defining your core values. Then, with those core values in mind, define the purpose of your practice."

You also said: "Next, envision a future where your practice is anchored to those core values and works toward achieving its purpose. Then, sit down with your staff and articulate a future that meets those criteria — one that you can feel in your gut just by speaking it. If it resonates on both the emotional level and the "I can and will achieve this" level, then you have a future that is possible."

You asked that I let you know how I did with that assignment.

Well I did it and it worked. Now I am scared because I haven't the faintest idea of what to do next. Can you help me again?

• ◦ •

Your next step is to build structures for fulfillment to make your future happen.

A structure for fulfillment transforms a possibility into a reality. The structure is based on this principle:

POSSIBILITY • OPPORTUNITY • RESULTS

So, the first step is to convert your possibility into an opportunity. A possibility is something that pulls you forward and excites. When you see it as possible, you are poised to take action. You are ready to go. But a possibility only creates the condition for action, it doesn't produce action. Now, you as a leader need to turn into you as a manager. A leader generates possibility. A manager generates action. That's the difference between a leader and a manager. As a manager, it's time to generate action.

How do you do that? How do you generate action? You make legitimate commitments.

What converts a possibility into an opportunity is commitment. Commitment is generated by making promises or requests. A request is asking another for a promise. Promises and requests increase in power the more specific and time-anchored they are. Promises made to yourself have little power. Promises made to another have much greater power. Promises use future-tense verbs. So, in essence, a promise commits you to a future where you make a stand that your word is law in the universe and you will do what it takes to make it happen.

So, here is your next step: Make specific promises — and requests — to your staff about what you will do in terms of actions and results. Those promises and requests must clearly demonstrate that you are climbing the mountain to reach your vision.

Then, go about fulfilling those promises.

TO INSPIRE, YOU HAVE TO ASPIRE

I have never been an inspiring leader. I have spent my time, paid my dues, gone to CE programs, read books, even hired coaches from time to time, but I still am unable to spark the kind of enthusiasm and excitement in my staff that I see others do.

For example, I recently returned from a program and I was incredibly enthusiastic. The speaker wasn't a particularly forceful speaker, but somehow was able to light a fire that left me burning to get out and get into action.

What's missing in my leadership that I can't inspire my staff? Am I missing the leadership gene?

• ◦ •

According to *Webster's New World Dictionary*, the word "inspire" means "to breathe life into." It also means "to cause, communicate or motivate as by divine influence." It's a very powerful word that paints a picture of something or someone beyond ourselves, infusing us with a purpose or a mission that calls us to act.

But what exactly is that "something else beyond ourselves" that has the power to infuse leaders to inspire others? What is that "something else" that consumes leaders with a genuine purpose or mission, so that when they speak, people are moved to commit and act? Whatever that "something beyond else" is, it's what is missing from your efforts to inspire your staff.

As you are well aware, one job of a leader is to generate a vision. A vision is not a future based on the past. Nor is a vision a future that is pie-in-the-sky. A vision is a future that the leader — and the people with whom the leader communicates — sees and feels is really possible.

There's another critical element of a vision that not only makes it powerful, but also enables the leader to inspire others. What is that element? That element is "service." The future that is expressed in a vision must in some way serve others.

A self-serving vision does not touch and move others. If the vision isn't in service to making things better for others, in this case, patients, it loses an element of the divine. And without that element of the divine, the leader may want, may wish and may hope, but he or she cannot aspire to make the vision real in the world.

It's those dentists who aspire to fulfill their visions, visions that serve their patients, who are most able to inspire their staffs. It's those dentists who aspire to serve other dentists through making their knowledge and vision fully accessible and compelling who are most effective in inspiring other dentists. It's those practice management consultants who aspire to serve their clients to become fully able business leaders, managers and owners who inspire their clients.

You see, for a number of dentists, dentistry simply provides them with a good job, a way to gain security and status. When you view dentistry as just a good job, you are not aspiring to serve anyone beyond yourself. If you're not aspiring, you're not able to inspire others.

So, my coaching is this: Create an authentic vision that serves others. A vision that would make a difference for people. A vision that would be worth putting yourself fully at stake for. A vision that the staff would hold as noble.

Then focus on your inspiration.

LOOKING FOR POSSIBILITY

Somehow I am not able to get my staff enthusiastic or excited about the future. I have figured out what I want to produce in the next year and the major projects I want to get done. However, when I talk to the staff about them, they give me that polite smile and nod their heads, but I know they aren't committed to getting it done.

What should I do?

• ∘ •

A better question to ask than "What should I do?" is "What is missing, the presence of which would ignite the staff to be excited and enthusiastic about the future?"

What is missing is *possibility*.

The way you are speaking about the future, your goals and projects, doesn't allow your staff to see what is possible when and if those goals and projects are accomplished.

Answer these questions:

What is the possibility for the practice if those things happen?

What is possible for our patients?

What is possible for each staff member if the goals are met and the projects accomplished?

What will it mean to them individually and collectively?

What is the possibility for me as an owner, as a manager and as a clinician if I achieve my goals?

New domains of possibility should open up if your goals and projects are achieved.

For example, what is possible for the staff if your revenue targets are accomplished? One certainty is an increase in their salaries. Another possibility is that in achieving the revenue goals, your staffers would need to operate more as a team. As a result, they should become more effective at their jobs. In addition, staff members would need to communicate more effectively to reach the revenue targets. So what is possible, if you reach your targets, is a championship team that works together incredibly well and fully supports and empowers each member. That's what's possible. And if your staff can see those possibilities, you'll get the job done.

Leaders speak of a future that is possible. Leaders speak of a future that others hear and see as possible. If people don't see possibility in a future, they hear it like a good idea. Nothing more. If there isn't possibility, there will be no excitement. If there isn't possibility, there will be no commitment. If there is no possibility, what will be present is resignation — in your case, polite resignation.

Possibility is special. Possibility is not the past. It is something new that can be seen, felt and envisioned, something that allows for a new future to emerge.

In the 1950s, lots of people talked in general, largely academic terms about putting a man on the moon. But when President Kennedy spoke such a future, he held it as truly possible and the people he spoke this future to saw it as possible as well. And each and every person who heard him saw what it would mean to America, to us as a people and to mankind. The possibility of a man on the moon was greatness for a nation, a validation of greatness and a legacy for our children.

If you listen, the difference between a windbag and a leader is the leader speaks of a future in a way that others see as possible.

YOU CAN'T MANAGE UNLESS YOU LEAD FIRST

I've had it! My front desk of three years just gave me notice. She's taking a job with a specialist downtown. It was only three months ago that I had my third practice management consultant in the office to work on staff management.

I've spent a heck of a lot of money on consultants and staff CE over the last seven years. I must have lost at least two months of production overall with these consultants and courses. With this particular consultant alone I lost five days of production over four months. That doesn't include how much time she spent on the phone with my staff or our weekly calls. What a waste.

I just can't get staff to deliver. Nothing seems to help. After a consultant leaves, it's good for a short while, then after a few months, it all goes back to sub-par performance. Staff keeps turning over. Staff keeps asking for more money. None of them seem to care.

I've done the communication thing, the programs, the consultants and all their manuals, policies, incentives, targets, goals, performance reviews, staff meetings, etc. etc. But none of it has made any difference.

I've had it with staff management. What is there left to do?

• ◦ •

This isn't about staff management. In fact it has nothing to do with management. It's about your leadership.

You need to realize you can't have effective management without successful leadership — and you're not delivering as a leader — period.

The only way to make this situation better is to hold up a mirror and take a very long, hard look at yourself. You are failing as a leader. You need to wake up to the fact you can't have effective, powerful management without strong leadership. Your staff is not the problem — you are. You are the source of why management continues to fail in your office.

No matter how good a job these consultants did, and most practice management consultants do a pretty good job, they were all doomed

90

to failure. It would be like putting a drop of yellow into a sea of green. Nothing would change. No matter what kind of management structures and communications they set up and put into your environment, they would fall short of your expectations.

First, you need to understand that staff doesn't want to be managed. Most talented people despise being managed. In fact, the more you manage people, the worse their performance. What's glaringly missing in your practice is you haven't created a practice that your staff really cares about. A practice that a staff really cares about doesn't require a lot of management.

You have failed to create a vision and goals that is both compelling and inspiring. And what you're left with is to push and prod your staff to perform. Domination, intimidation, manipulation, and fear just aren't great management tools. You haven't generated a powerful purpose or an inspirational mission that challenges, generates enthusiasm or inspires.

I've read a lot of books on "What makes great companies great." I've gone to many business programs, attended graduate training programs at prestigious schools like Harvard and Wharton over the last two decades, as well as having had some world class mentors and Fortune 100 clients. While these books, teachers, clients and pundits disagree on a few salient points, not one of them ever cited excellent management as a significant influence on what makes companies great. Not one!

Without exception, extraordinary companies, great companies have a *compelling reason for being.* Microsoft with changing the world, Service Master with doing God's work, Progressive with revolutionizing insurance claims, or my own consulting company with having clients becoming extraordinary businessmen and businesswomen. Whether big or small, great companies are obsessed with achieving their vision — staying on purpose — accomplishing their mission.

When these obsessions drive companies, employees need few directives, reminders or motivational speeches. Simply put, these companies organize themselves around a compelling purpose — and work relentlessly to achieve it.

You can feel this quality when you walk into these companies' lobbies or these practices' waiting rooms. You can see it in the way people talk to each other in the halls. The lunch room echoes with a low roar with frequent laughter. These places are alive, buzzing with high energy. What would I experience walking into your practice for the morning huddle? How does the staff talk about the practice in your lunch room — if they do at all? If I asked your staff "What is the mission of this practice," what would they say? Are you passionately declaring and living a vision for the practice? Do you even have a vision?

My feeling is you are vastly under performing as a leader. Stop trying to fix management. Fix yourself as a leader.

SERVICE & THE NEW LEADERSHIP

I am at my wits-end. I haven't had a staff that works well together, performs well or is loyal to their jobs for a long time. I have been in practice 14 years and there have been only a few times that I can remember when the staff actually worked well and worked together. Most of the time they play politics, act to protect their own turf, are sassy and cynical, and always seem at odds with each other.

I hired a coach a couple months ago, and her advice was to be a tough, no nonsense boss and lay down the law. Since then, I've lost two staff people and two more are threatening to quit.

Now I have no idea what to do. I have no idea of what kind of leadership I should provide. I'm confused. At first I was a wimp and that didn't work. Now I am a tough and unmovable leader and that isn't working either.

What should I do?

• • •

From my point of view, you're way off base. It's the old brand of leadership. Your style of leadership is based on a military model that was firmly established during the industrial revolution; a charismatic individual leading the charge to achieve the mission.

Wake up. We are now in the tail end of the information age not in the industrial age. The Internet, instant information, globalization, and outsourcing. *This isn't Kansas any more.*

Unfortunately, the classic type of leadership is still being espoused by most pundits and consultants in dentistry. This form of hierarchical, top-down, command and control leadership, has used up its future and now has no future. This kind of leadership is going bankrupt in today's world and dentistry is extremely slow to acknowledge it.

I fully recognize that dentistry still worships the hero-leader as evidenced by the dental journals plastering some individual's face on it, adoring him as a leader who makes great things happen. Take a look at the covers of

Dentistry Today, Dental Town or Dental Economics. A full body shot, with a dentist in front of his modern practice building, staring dreamingly off into space. Then the article opens with him surrounded by his doting staff. The article goes into great depth about how he achieved his meteoric rise to become a dental superstar. Napoleon without the uniform. Washington leading his troops across the Delaware. Patton leading his tanks against the enemy. The commander and chief. That's our current image of leadership in dentistry today.

You need to be aware we are in a new age and a new context and dentistry resides within this new context — and context is decisive. Whoever your teachers and mentors are, whoever your role models are in leadership, they aren't keeping up with the times. What is clearly emerging as the most effective form of leadership is servant-leadership.

You see, to be a successful leader in the future, you will need to reach into the deepest part of human nature in order to inspire a staff member to rise above their own individual concerns, their own personal circumstances, and their seemingly petty day-to-day problems. As a leader you will need to appeal to the core of each of your staff, because when you tap into this source of human motivation, you rouse the staff to high performance.

Developing this ability to tap into the core of your staff's human spirit will require you to be (become) a servant-leader. The knowledge and skills needed to become a servant leader are not what people in dentistry are talking about. They're still harping on the same old stuff about leadership. Sorry folks, "the same old is the same old" and it simply won't carry the day.

Most dentists are not servant-leaders but rather self-serving leaders. They lead the staff for one purpose, to make sure the staff gets their jobs done so the dentist himself or herself will be successful. "The staff works for me. I sign their paychecks. They know who butters their bread."

Self-serving leaders lead by order and command, using threat, manipulation, money, favoritism or anything else they can get their hands on to make the staff do their bidding. The self-serving leader manages by and for control. But there is a cost.

Control always displaces trust. Control produces a low-trust culture. Low-trust cultures are characterized by dictatorial management, political posturing, protectionism, cynicism, internal competition and adversarialism (sound familiar?). The higher level of control you apply to your staff, the lower level of trust results, which then requires you to apply even more control, which further displaces trust — a perfect vicious cycle. All this leads to poor staff performance, poor quality outcomes, lack of team and no innovation. No wonder dentistry has one of the highest turnover rates of any industry. No wonder many of your staff are jumping ship.

You can buy someone's hands and back, but you can't buy their heart, mind and spirit. And without your staff's heart, mind and spirit you won't stimulate your their creative talent, commitment and loyalty. The hardest part for you will be giving up your traditional, high control, top down management.

The term servant-leadership was first coined in a 1970 essay by Robert K. Greenleaf. Over his 25 years of consulting, after a 40-year career as a senior executive with ATT, Greenleaf taught and consulted major companies such as MIT, Ford Foundation, R.K. Mellon Foundation, GE and many others. I had the unique opportunity to spend two days of training and development with the then 88-year old Mr. Greenleaf in 1987. Mr. Greenleaf was truly a remarkable human being. He left an indelible mark.

Greenleaf's main belief about what is central to leadership is the great leaders first experience themselves as a servant to others, and that this simple fact of being "in service to others" is central to his or her greatness as a leader. "True leadership emerges from the primary motivation to help others."

My work with clients is to have them develop the skills to become a servant-leader. I'll list these skills below. I can't go into detail on these skills. The first evening of my "Putting the Service Back in Fee-For-Service Workshop" is just with the docs to work on being a servant-leader and developing these skills. Here are the skills you need to develop to be a successful servant-leader.

- Listening

- Empathy (Recreation)

- Self Awareness

- Enrollment

- Context Creation (Conceptualization)

- Foresight (Future/Vision)

- Stewardship

- Commitment to Growing People

My recommendation is for you to learn more about servant-leader. We've all heard the phrase, "Ride the horse in the direction it's going." In my world-view, the direction is clearly servant-leader.

WHY CAN'T I KEEP STAFF?

I suffer from high staff turnover and can't seem to find or keep good people. I use a well-tested interview process. I do a probationary period. I do performance reviews. I pay on the high end of the scale. I have a generous bonus system. I have staff meetings. I do a lot of things to keep staff.

In addition, I have been through some practice management programs so I have a vision, a budget, targets and goals. I have top-of-the-line equipment, computers and digital gear and I am in a great location.

I have never had a staff stay together and perform at the top level.

What's the problem?

•   ·   •

The problem is you.

If you are willing to confront that problem, take responsibility for it, own up to it and do something about it, you can change your situation. If not, nothing will change. It's up to you. It's your call.

The place where you are failing is in your leadership. And by the way, that is not an uncommon problem with dentists. There is a part of your leadership that is missing. Although you have a vision for the future of the practice, and may have even spoken to the staff about it so they can see it and own it, that is only one part of leadership.

The part you're missing is critical and fundamental. In my work I call it "source." You are not relating to your staff their worth and potential in a way that they can see their worth and potential in themselves. Leaders who cannot generate that interaction usually fail. It's the kind of leadership that powerfully influences and endures. Successful leaders communicate the potential and worth to staff so clearly, so powerfully and so consistently that staff members come to see themselves in that way.

But that means you need to see the potential and worth in each staff member. And that, my friend, is where the transformation needs to start, because right now you don't. You don't see your staff's potential. You don't recognize their worth. You see them as objects to be pushed and pulled to get the job done. Your first job is to recognize and be aware that you hold staff as "things." You may be thinking, "I pay them a good salary. They have good jobs. They only work four days a week and I pay them like five. They owe it to me to do their jobs."

When you hold that someone owes you, you totally lack appreciation. Therefore, you lack appreciation for staff and what they do for you. Relationships that lack appreciation are short-term. No one stays in a relationship where he or she is not appreciated.

When you think someone owes you, you come from "I deserve." So you walk around your practice with an attitude of "I deserve" for staff to do their jobs, not complain and get along.

If you follow the "they owe me" track to "I deserve," the next rung on the ladder is "I expect." You expect them to perform. I'd bet your expectations are rarely if ever communicated. You just expect. Expectations are never negotiated. You just expect. And unfulfilled expectations cause upsets. So you end up being constantly upset with your staff.

Who wants to work for an upset boss?

If I were your coach, I'd have you work in your practice for just two days without thinking your staff owes you something. I'd have you cut out believing you deserve. I'd have you voice your expectations and negotiate them with each staff member. That's where we'd start.

Then I'd coach and counsel you on how to acknowledge people so staff feel known, honored and appreciated. Once we got to that point, it would be a straight shot to assisting you in seeing how to recognize and acknowledge their worth and potential. But when you have the trifocal lenses on of "owe, deserve and expect," you can't see people for who they are and, therefore, can't see their potential and worth.

FLIPPING WITHOUT FLOPPING

I am afraid to pull the trigger on hiring another assistant. Some days it looks like a must, other days it looks like a waste of money. I can't decide. All kinds of considerations keep on coming up — more management, more problems, more salary and so on.

Some months we have great production, and during those times we really need another hand. Other months we don't have the production and adding an assistant seems stupid. The staff keeps on bugging me and asking when we are going to hire another assistant. I keep telling them I'm working on it.

But hiring an assistant isn't the only thing I can't make up my mind about. Equipment purchases, marketing, even waiting room furniture — I can't decide. Why am I so indecisive? Why can't I make up my mind and just follow through? I feel like my flip-flopping means that I stink as a leader.

I need some advice!

• • •

Somehow you have the view that to be an effective leader you need to be absolutely and unconditionally decisive. You think, as many dentists do, that you need to take swift and sure action and then remain steadfast, no matter what. It seems the worst thing anyone can do is change his or her mind.

What you now believe is that the ultimate failure as a leader is to flip-flop. In my view, that is very, very troublesome, because leaders need to be able to flip-flop without fear.

Flip-flopping is not the same thing as indecision. Indecision is the inability to arrive at a choice. Flip-flopping is altering your stance after a choice has been made. Changing course is the right move in many circumstances.

As a leader, you should flip when you realize you have made the wrong decision. I am old enough to remember Ronald Reagan denouncing the Soviet Union as the evil empire ruled by ruthless leaders. He flipped and worked with Gorbachev to bring an end to the Cold War. Over the years, my clients have continually pressed me to produce a conference and I always refused. The Mastery Conference is now an annual event delivered on both coasts.

I understand that staff responds to the leader's declarations and takes action depending on what the leader says. If the leader changes his or her mind, and the staff has already made commitments based on a previous decision, that could cause the staff to be upset. If the leader does an about-face, the basis for the staff's decisions collapses. I appreciate any leader's concern about flipping because of the impact on staff or what the staff might think. But what if you don't flip and it has very deleterious, long-term effects on the business?

So I appreciate the difficulty in making decisions in tough economic circumstances and the impact it has on the staff. You're afraid you'll get stuck with more staff than you need and, once decided, you won't be able to change the situation.

Like most dentists, you want to appear strong, resolute, unwavering — a John Wayne kind of leader. And since your decisions are shared events with the staff, you feel you can't flip. The announcement, the strong justification, your noble answer to the challenge makes reversing course even more difficult. You are afraid you won't look good.

Good leaders know they always need the option to re-decide. When I train and coach leaders, I ask that they always prepare the way for reversals. They need to send a direct message to staff that they aren't afraid to take a second look at any decision and to change their minds if they see something won't work or will be harmful to patients or their practices.

Changing your mind doesn't mean you are unable to lead. In my view, changing your mind says you have an ability to learn. Changing your mind is not a sin. It's just a way of saying you're wiser today than you were yesterday.

If you knew you could change your mind after you hired an additional assistant if it didn't work out, what would you do?

WHAT REALLY MATTERS IN BEING SUCCESSFUL

I've been moderately successful in a practice I began eight years ago. But to date, I haven't been able to break through the barrier to become highly successful. I have completed programs and courses. I've spent time and money with consultants. I have all the stuff I'm supposed to have — including the latest clinical, optical and computer gear. I even used an office decorator who specializes in feng shui. I make sure we do the high-tech, high-touch. I have the scripts. I have a fairly good staff. Even with all of that, I am not realizing the success that some other dentists do.

What do you suppose I am missing?

. . .

Success in the long run has little to do with finding the best models, setting up the finest organizational structures, adopting the top business practices, having the latest and greatest equipment or becoming a pre-eminent clinician. It has much more to do with discovering what really matters to you.

Until you discover what really matters to you, you will not be really successful. What really matters to you is core. It is there, at the very core level, where thought and feeling inform each other. It is when you are in touch with what really matters to you, when creativity is at its highest. It's where real power emerges.

I've only worked with a couple of thousand dentists, so my sample size, client mix and the dentists who are attracted to my work might skew my perception. You need to take what I say with a grain of salt. In terms of personality, my clients are all over the map. Some are loud and assertive. Some are barely audible. Some are charismatic, many are not. But the dentists who are most successful, no matter what their personalities, light up when you ask them what really matters to them.

What I have found in working with successful dentists is that each one, in his or her own way, found him- or herself on a collision course with a deep need, a need that generated a relentless, passionate conviction to change the way things are done in dental practice and dentistry. That conviction to change the way things are done in dental practice is expressed in spite of how their colleagues, their profession or even society judged them.

I have observed that highly successful practitioners don't rely on the approval of others to pursue their callings or causes. They have the audacity to take the initiative despite social and professional pressures. Bottom Line: They are unconditionally committed to doing what they love, more than being loved by others. Dentists like that don't wallow in or obsess about defeat or failure. Nor do they seek scapegoats to blame when things go wrong.

So, ask yourself what really matters to you as a dentist and in your dental practice. What are you unconditionally committed to expressing, achieving, representing, studying and mastering? Are you on the path to acting on and accomplishing what matters to you? If not, my assertion is you won't ever be really successful.

Another quality I consistently find in dentists with long-standing success is they are "builders." In the book *Built to Last* by Collins and Porras, the authors talk about "clock builders." It is a metaphor they use to distinguish between the ability to tell the time at the moment and the ability to build a clock that can tell time beyond the lifetime of the builder. Dentists who are "builders" create a vision and practice culture that significantly outperforms the practices of time-tellers.

Builders are dentists who feel compelled to create something new or better in their practices. They build practices that will endure throughout their lifetimes and beyond. In fact, I have discovered that practice transitions that succeed tend to have "builder" senior dentists. And practice transitions that fail are owned and operated by time-tellers. Is that the real key to successful transitions?

Builders see themselves simply as people committed to making a difference — doing something with their practices that needs to be done — with or without them. With that as their perspective, they hire staff, build infrastructures and go about their business with a "making a difference" mind-set.

My Message: You have it within in you to have a highly successful practice.

My Coaching: Fully embrace a personally meaningful journey, integrating your personal and professional life and building something that will make a lasting difference, a practice that lasts and that will outlast you.

CORE VALUES: TRUE OR FALSE

You have been talking about core values. I am taking on a new associate soon and I recall that one of your recommendations was that the senior dentist and incoming dentist both agree on their core values. I think I know what my core values are, but how can I really be certain?

• ○ •

I work with lots of associateships and partnerships and my starting point is always core values. Why? Because when the core values are not aligned or the core values are violated, the relationship always breaks down. Always! No amount of accommodation by either party will eliminate the damage done when a core value is dishonored. Once this occurs, the relationship begins to unravel and is very difficult to restore.

But your question is how do I know my core values are "real" core values? Here's our formula for assuring your core values are really core values.

CORE VALUES • COMMITMENTS • MONEY TIME • ENERGY

To make sure you have accurately defined your core values, write down those values you unconditionally honor, those things you hold sacrosanct — integrity, quality, excellence, fairness, etc.

Now step back and take stock of your day-to-day actions. You might notice a gap between the things you say you really value and the way you actually spend your time, money and energy. Any gap raises questions about the authenticity of your core values.

Core values ought to be unconditional guides to commitments you make everyday in the practice. Commitments generate actions taken in the present that bind you and your practice to a future. It might be you closing down a third of your practice one day, totally disengaging from all your PPO relations with your insurance companies, going strictly fee-for-service.

I am talking about those commitments that are mundane as to be almost invisible. For example, you purchase a particular kind of implant and really like it. Over time it becomes your implant system of choice. You feel comfortable with these fixtures. You are using it nearly all the time. Results are pretty good. Soon the implant company seduces you into being a spokesperson for them which further locks you into this implant system. Although you might claim one of your core values is "excellence," since you are now locked into using only one kind of implant, you won't use another type to see if you can produce even a better result with your patients. Those unexamined commitments you made along the way don't support your declared core value. In fact, they demonstrate just the opposite.

Or you might be a seasoned specialist who concentrates his marketing effort on his key referrals — those referrals that send you lots of cases. However, one of those key referrals does less than ethical dentistry, but since he supplies you with a very high number of new patients, you continues to market to him. Although you declare one of your core values as "optimum dental care," your time, your actions and your energy don't reflect this core value.

Another example is you might claim the "Golden Rule" as a core value. "Do unto others….treat staff like we would like to be treated ourselves…..etc." Nevertheless, you gossip about your hygienist with your office manager. You're not walking the talk.

So do some reverse engineering. Keep the core values you wrote down in front of you. Now honestly look at where you spend your energy, time and money. This will reveal your commitments. Since commitments are a direct expression of your true core values, look closely at your commitments and be honest about what are your true core values.

ENERGY · MONEY · TIME
COMMITMENTS · CORE VALUES

When your energy, time, money, your commitments, and your core values all line up — that's when your core values are truly operational. That's when you have integrity with your core values. When your core values, your commitments, your time, money and energy all are aligned — you will be empowered.

Some dentists declare core values that they think they should have, such as quality, excellence, fairness. By doing the exercise described above, you will reveal whether your declared core values are truthful or phony. If accurate, great, if phony, dump them. Or if you feel they truly are your core values and you have been violating them — clean up your act.

HOW DO I KNOW IF I'M DOING A VISION PROPERLY?

I have been working on my vision and strategy. It's not the first time I have done so. But how do I know if I am doing it right? How do I know that what I am developing and articulating is a vision and a correct strategy? Last time I did something similar, it didn't seem to make much difference.

• • •

Most planning that dentists do around their businesses involves incremental change. Grow it 10% here, save 2% there, increase new patients by four a month, paint the waiting room a different color, get a digital camera, install a monitor in each operatory. All those efforts make little difference in the scheme of things.

And so, not surprisingly, dentists begin their "vision" thinking in that place as well. "Given what I know, a 5.4% revenue growth target makes sense." Logical. Sensible. Affordable. Not much risk. Keeps on paying the bills. It is an extrapolation from what is current, known and considered doable.

Most dentists generate their vision and strategies by asking a particular set of questions that doesn't stimulate the thinking, imagination or creativity that produces powerful visions or bold strategies. They ask questions based on reducing the risk, keeping themselves comfortable and allowing themselves to maintain the status quo.

Dentists generally don't begin the process by asking questions like, "What does it mean to be a $10 million practice?" "What does it mean to create a leading-edge cosmetic practice that is top-of-the-rank?" "How do I develop a new kind of dental practice for adolescents and young adults, given the market that sub-population is, along with its distinctive needs and concerns?" "How do I become the leading implant practice in my region?" Those are questions about non-incremental change — as opposed to questions based on financial analysis, small alterations and commonly accepted assumptions.

A vision is a bold view of the future that you and your practice have and that you feel in your gut is possible. It's a future that you know you can commit to achieving. It's a future that you are willing to take risks to achieve. It's a future based not on the past. It is a future that isn't based on your current identity or ego. It is a future that will make a difference for others.

So the riddle of vision is this:

> *A vision is a future in a future, about a future, for a future,*
> *not based on the past, not about you, that people see and feel*
> *is possible, that you are committed to achieving.*

If your vision meets those criteria, it is a true vision.

A vision is a declaration. Declarations are powerful speech acts — but you can only declare something that is a match for who you think you are in the world. For example, Henry Ford said, "I'll make a car that everyone can afford to drive." Declaring a similarly remarkable vision would require you to believe that you are a remarkable person able to take on the challenges and risks of realizing your vision.

That is the power of vision. It allows you to pull yourself up by your own bootstraps, to be bigger and bolder than you realize you are, to take greater risks and ultimately to produce far greater results.

You need to reflect on who you consider yourself to be and on whether you are willing to challenge fundamental assumptions about yourself. Are you willing to declare a vision that you hold as possible, that you will commit to achieving, that will alter the future of you and your practice along with it?

DON'T LEAD BY RESULTS.
LEAD FOR RESULTS

What I have been led to believe, from what I've read and from the two nationally recognized consultants that I've worked with, I should have my staff stay focused on the financial goals of the practice. As I understand it, if I can get my staff focused on the financial outcomes, I will naturally increase my financial results.

So for the last year, I have been trying very hard to get the staff to pay close attention to the financial results and financial goals of the practice. I've been trying to press upon them the importance of making our financial targets.

Each week I review the monthly and weekly financial performance. In fact, to keep my staff focused on the financial results, I've developed a bonus system based on collections. I've put up the production and collection numbers, cumulative and daily results, in the staff lunch room on a white board, which we update every day. I constantly let them know that if we don't make our numbers, we can't pay them more money.

The problem is the financial goals we set are not being met. The staff's morale is at an all-time low. How can I get them to pay attention to the financial targets of the practice? How can I get them to be committed to making our financial targets? Am I doing something wrong?

• ⁕ •

Yes, in my view, you are doing something wrong.

It always interests me to ask this question: "Why do you pound the financial results so hard into your staff?" In my experience, it rarely, if ever, produces the desired result. Now, I'm not saying the other consultants are wrong. I'm just saying that in all my experience in practice management I've never seen it really work.

I believe the way you are presenting the financial goals and the financial results is causing a certain interpretation by your staff — an interpretation that directly and powerfully poses a significant risk to the success of your practice. When a dentist tells the staff, "We must focus all our attention on our financial results," staff usually interprets it to mean, "Do whatever we need to do to make money!"

The problem is you and the staff become fully wrapped up in the financial results and, therefore, lose sight of the connection between behavior, in the form of action, and results. When you focus only on the numbers, you omit learning opportunities. And worse, you overlook building long-term value in the practice.

Some consulting colleagues I know truly believe the only purpose of a dentist's leadership is to make aggressive predictions and promises about quarterly, monthly and daily results. They encourage dentists and staff members to go about achieving the numbers by any means necessary. In my experience, that is a big mistake. What the staff hears is this: "These are the results I have to have. I don't care how you get it done." That ends up costing a lot more than the results are worth.

That "do or die for the money" interpretation is then reinforced by your bonus system. It motivates the staff to more narrowly focus their attention and actions on making the numbers — period.

In my view, financial results are a function of three distinct, yet highly interrelated, elements: intelligent strategy, an incessant focus on quality of execution and an obsessive focus on customer service.

Here's an analogy: Tiger Woods's best bet for winning a major championship is mastering his aim, setup and swing. Once the ball is in the air, there is no way to control it. In other words, when the financial results happen, it's already too late to impact them. It's already a done deal.

By using financial results as a diagnostic tool in the service of improving execution and by asking your staff to participate in the analysis and give recommendations, financial results are much more useful.

I'll bet the way you use financial results is more like a whip, which is, of course, producing an undesired effect. What does it feel like in your office when you don't achieve your financial results? Does it feel to your staff as though they've failed? As a leader, is that the mood and attitude you want to create? Are you making the staff dissatisfied and grouchy? Is that the outcome you want to produce? Keep on pressuring the staff with the numbers and you'll keep on getting what you are getting: zero improvement.

How do you think patients react to a grouchy, dissatisfied and irritable staff? How many new patients will they refer? How much high-end dentistry will they accept?

Now, I am not saying you shouldn't manage by the numbers. I am saying you should use the numbers in a different way. Use them as a way to learn, to understand, to improve. Don't use your numbers to flog yourself and your staff. Use your numbers to improve performance, to improve quality, to improve patient word-of-mouth marketing. Don't use your numbers as a hammer.

The way you are most likely using your numbers makes it personal. You are indirectly saying to your staff, "You aren't good enough." You are assigning blame and fault, implicitly stating, "If you really did your jobs, we'd make our financial targets." Wake up! You are disempowering your staff. You're making it worse, not better.

My Coaching: Use your financial numbers to learn what to do better, to identify what's not working, to measure improvement. If you can talk about your numbers in that way, the subject will move from the subjective to the objective. And in management, you get a lot more from people when you're objective.

TO FAIL IS HUMAN,
TO QUIT IS DISASTER

I have been in practice for six years and I still can't make any money. I can't keep staff. I never have good months consecutively. I feel I am failing and I am a failure. My colleagues are all making money and doing well.

I am really worried about my practice. What's wrong?

• • •

You keep this up and you won't have to worry about your practice, because you won't have one.

I can tell you what's missing, but I can't generate it. I can point to what you need, but I can't do it. If it were up to me I would, but it's not — it's up to you. Your relationship to failure is typical of many dentists. "If at first you don't succeed, give up."

You are resigned, so the mood of the practice is "resignation." Resignation always displaces "possibility." And what leadership provides is a genuine sense of possibility. So what's missing in your practice big-time is leadership.

Do you wonder why your staff underperforms and leaves? Because you're resigned. Nothing kills high performance and commitment faster than resignation. Resignation is a "virus." You are the host. It spreads rapidly. It becomes an epidemic, infecting each and every staff member.

The question you need to ask yourself is: "How do I shift my world view from resignation to possibility?"

The Answer: "You alter your relationship to failure."

Failure is something I am very intimate with. I am an expert on failure. I've had many big, and public, failures in my life. Both in my practice and in my consulting career. Huge. Mega. Embarrassing. Costly. Really big ones! But I am in very good company. The striking thing about most successful people is how often they have failed. Turn on a light, take a photograph, watch television, search the Web, jet across the Pacific, talk on a cell phone. The people who left us these legacies had to find their way to "Eldorado" through a maze of wrong turns.

Last month we celebrated the 125th anniversary of Thomas Edison's success in heating a spiral of carbonized cotton for 14 hours in his lab in New Jersey. Three years later Edison went on to light up half a square mile of Manhattan. What he said about failure was, "Many of life's failures are people who did not realize how close they were to success when they gave up." And this is the certainly the guy to make this statement. After 3,000 experiments about electric light, each of them reasonable and most likely true, only in two cases did Edison's experiment work.

The lesson here is "You only fail when you quit."

The most common quality to success is persistence. Success only comes with an emotional resilience of character to deal with failure. At one point Walt Disney was so broke after a succession of financial flops that he was stranded shoeless in his office because he couldn't afford the $1.50 to reclaim his shoes at the repair shop.

In our culture, particularly dentistry, failures are hidden. In the dental industry, our magazines, journals and myths have a way of reporting on the process of trial and error so that only the peaks are shown, not the valleys.

We teach, preach and coach that "breakdowns are the only access to the future." If our clients can see that failures are clearly the access to success, they won't be ashamed of them, they won't try to hide them, and they won't be covert about them. I strongly suggest you stop feeling sorry for yourself. Stop being the victim.

My recommendation is straightforward. Generate a powerful and inspiring mission. Then your profit center is your passion center and your vocation and avocation will be the same.

CONTEXT OF MANAGEMENT

MANAGEMENT has two jobs: getting work done through people and developing people through work.

MANAGEMENT gets work done through others by focusing on outcomes and results.

Results are a function of integrity and structure. MANAGEMENT'S job is, therefore, to encourage people to give and keep their word — integrity — and ensure that they do so. Then, management builds structures to make that happen. Those structures include systems, goals, targets, metrics, feedback mechanisms, manuals, job descriptions, performance reviews, training and coaching.

MANAGEMENT communicates in three basic languages. One is commitment. In it, people give their word about what they'll do and by when they'll do it. Management's job is to empower them to keep their promises.

The second language of MANAGEMENT is coaching. It is a way of communicating that enhances the effectiveness of the actions people take in doing their jobs.

And the third language management speaks is acknowledgement. That way people are known, honored and appreciated.

MANAGEMENT'S job is also to develop people through work. Management does that by increasing the scope and depth of people's promises so a gap is created, requiring them to expand their skills and abilities in order to close it.

MANAGEMENT'S duty is to continuously format the complexity of delivering the final service or product into do-able units that can be achieved by employees so the patient/customer is fully served.

Ultimately, MANAGEMENT gets paid for results.

TACKLING STAFF BEHAVIOR

One thing I do that I know I shouldn't do is fail to address issues with my staff immediately. I wait until something gets so bad that I am forced to act. Even though I know I should talk to the staff member as soon as I recognize the problem, I don't.

Why do I keep on doing this?

• ○ •

First, I appreciate your question. It is an affliction of most dentists, nearly all of whom are conflict-averse. Let's take Dr. John, for example. He fears that if he confronts an issue, it will cause a conflict. So, being conflict-averse, he avoids addressing the issue altogether.

Rather than handling a staff issue when it occurs, Dr. John hopes it will simply go away. "Hope" is the operative word here. In management, hope never works.

There are several ways for you to improve your performance in this area. First, get very clear on the benefits and the costs of your current behavior.

Are you really aware of the depth and magnitude of the costs? It costs you your own well-being. It costs you the respect of the other staff members. It costs you better staff performance and, therefore, time and money. It costs you your self-worth, your power, and your future. When you really get in touch with the costs you will see that they are usually very high.

What you may not be aware of are the benefits of continuing your current behavior. You may not see the payoff in avoiding the issues. You actually get a lot out of not addressing the issues with staff.

So what are the benefits? You get to play it safe. You don't have to take a risk and put the issue on the table. Another benefit is you can make your staff members wrong and have yourself be right. "She's [fill in the blank]." "He just doesn't [fill in the blank]." Worse, you may go around to other staff members and get agreement about why you are right, which is just another form of gossip. A third benefit is you don't have to be responsible. Why? Because it's his or her fault. And remember, the antithesis of responsibility is blame, guilt and fault. So it's a good way to get yourself off the hook. And lastly, you don't have to fulfill your commitments as a leader, owner or manager.

Because you are unaware of the benefits, you'll wait until the costs are so crushing that you have to do something about it. But, by that time the situation is usually so bad and toxic it requires a huge amount of energy and time — or you are left with only one action: "You're fired."

These benefits are inherently more important to you than practice success and staff performance. They are more important to you than your core values and your commitments. These benefits are more important to you than making your targets or goals. You'd rather be right than happy. Your behavior can only change when you realize the costs are greater than the benefits and that the benefits actually sabotage your success.

So Step 1 is realizing that the reason you are afraid to confront your staff is you are scared to make yourself responsible and take a risk. You don't want to give up being right. It's much easier to avoid being direct and straightforward. And you make it okay to not be a powerful owner, leader and manager because you think that your real job is being a dentist.

Step 2 is doing it.

HOW DO I MAKE MY STAFF CARE?

I want my staff to be more effective, more accountable, more responsible. Seems I am the only one, with the exception of my business manager, who really cares. How do I get my staff to be more responsible?

• · •

Here's the bad news: You can't "make" anyone responsible. You can't lay responsibility on someone. Responsibility is taken, never given.

What I mean by responsibility is holding yourself accountable. You must see yourself as the agent that produced the circumstance, issue or problem. Blame, shame, guilt and fault are the opposite of responsibility. When you blame someone, you are not making him or her responsible.

Responsibility begins with choice, so that is where I would begin with your staff: putting them at choice. To do that, you need to make a direct, clear request and let them know they have the choice of saying "Yes" or "No." Either response has a consequence.

For example, say a staff member is becoming consumed with a personal matter. She is now constantly on the phone trying to work it out. Worse, this is a long-term problem with a family member. There are many times you walk out to the front desk and rather than seeing her with patients or on the phone with patients, you see her on the phone with people involved in her family matter. She is an experienced employee who usually gets the job done.

What do you do?

You sit her down and put her at choice. The practice needs attention and intention. The patients, schedule and other issues need attention and intention. The staff member has neither. If you hope it is going to get better, you'll be disappointed. Hope does not work as a management technique.

The conversation is straightforward. Here are the basics:

"This is what the practice needs to operate. I am not getting that from you. I understand you have concerns and issues. I appreciate your problems. I am not sure what you need to do to make your situation better. But the practice has needs and requirements. So I need for you to make a choice about how you want to be in the practice. It's up to you. Choose. I am willing to support you in whatever choice you make."

"Yes" takes it in one direction. "No" takes it in another. So rather than dictating correction, rather than making demands or, if you are like most dentists, delivering covert communications, make clear requests and give people the opportunity to make choices. You know what you need. They can say "Yes" to it or "No" to it. It's up to them, not you.

HIGH TEST GAS BUT NO ACCELERATION

I have been in general practice for 16 years. I have spent a lot of money developing my practice systems, structures and software. I have also used consultants and trainers to assist me in developing and implementing those systems and structures. I try to stay on the forefront. Last year I changed my software, which has been a terrible nightmare, but I thought it would really improve the practice's performance in numbers of areas.

I have always believed that with those investments — upgrading my business systems and structures — my practice would grow at a significant rate. It hasn't. Yet, I don't know what else to do to increase the performance of the practice.

What's my problem?

• ◦ •

I know you'd like to believe what you read in the dental rags about a practice's success depending on strategy, structure and systems. I know it's easy to sit in an audience as the dental gurus talk about business structures and systems and be swayed into buying their brand of snake oil. It's not that systems and structures aren't important. They are. But as with a car, the performance is a lot more dependent on the driver than the vehicle itself.

You hear this all the time: "Get the right business plan. Have a functional budget. Generate up-to-date employee manuals. Do routine staff performance reviews. Set clear targets and goals. Get the latest and greatest software." And on and on. Those recommendations are being pitched as "The Answer." But they are only a part of the answer and, clearly, are not the answer itself.

News Flash! Having the best structures and systems does little if anything to enhance practice performance. Sorry. It's a myth. Looks like you bought into the myth. Peak performance has much more to do with communication than snake oil. But dentists keep on throwing money at better systems and expensive advice on developing and managing better systems, software and structures. Sometime I wonder why dentists just don't just burn their money. It's quicker.

Here's my advice: *Learn how to communicate effectively.* Learn how to initiate crucial and difficult conversations. Learn how to communicate at the right time, in the right place, with the right person. And watch your productivity soar!

Check this out. Look at what happens when you or your employees fail to deliver on your promises. In the most successful practices I work with, when people don't deliver on their promises, someone steps in to discuss the problem. In underperforming or failing practices, no one says a word. The conversation is avoided. How does it work in your practice?

In good practices, dentists deal directly and immediately with problems. In the best practices, everyone holds everyone accountable, regardless of his or her level or position. The path to high performance doesn't pass through a static system, but through face-to-face effective communication at all levels.

The most productive and profitable practices I have worked with have developed the skills to effectively deal with difficult or crucial conversations rather than avoid or bypass them.

Ask yourself this: If an employee is underperforming, fails to live up to a promise, doesn't carry his or her fair share of the weight or isn't productive enough, are you able as a practice to address the issue right away? If not, therein lies your productivity problem.

Here is my recommendation. Read one or all three of the following books:
- *Fierce Conversations* (Scott)
- *Difficult Conversations* (Stone, Patton, Heen)
- *Crucial Conversations* (Patterson)

Work on communication and you will produce and maintain positive relationships in your office and dramatically decrease your turnover rate. Get trained in effective communication. Get someone in your office who knows how to improve your communication.

Bottom Line: Communicating Better = Making More Money!

I NEED A STAFF WAKEUP CALL

I have great difficulty in being direct with my staff. There are things I want to say that I don't say. I see people do things that upset me and I don't address them. I step around them or avoid them all together.

What should I do?

. . .

Dentists, more than any other professionals, have trouble communicating. In fact, it is exactly that difficulty that is often a major contributing factor in pushing them into dentistry, because it is a structural interaction, not a communicative interaction. In other words, it is easier to work on teeth than talk to people.

It's only natural that you should gravitate to where there is the least discomfort. In dentistry, the discomfort in communication is much deeper and broader with staff people than with patients or colleagues. Therefore, you must first realize that you will be doing something that makes you uncomfortable and you must realize that it will require you to take a risk to do it.

So the first question is: "Are you willing to take the risk?" If the answer is, "No," send a memo, hope or complain. Those won't work, of course, but they'll make you feel better. If the answer is, "Yes, I am willing to take a risk," then continue reading.

Now, stop rehearsing what you are going to say in your head. It never comes out that way. You are not going to do it "right." In fact, there is no "right" way to do it. There is only "doing it."

Here is a special technique for doing that. The technique has three steps. You must follow all three in the recommended order. No skipping to the end!

STEP 1: *Confess or disclose your feelings or your fears.*
To get the communication started, you need to get yourself on the field of honest communication. So you first must reveal how what you are about to say makes you feel.

Example: "I am really uncomfortable talking to you about this particular issue and I have been avoiding talking about it for three months." By honestly reporting how the communication makes you feel, you will create a relationship and a condition where you can say what you have to say. Remember, do not skip any step.

STEP 2: *Tell the staff member what you are afraid he or she will think, say or do if you say it.*
One major reason you don't say what you want to say is you are afraid of the conflict or upset it will cause. You hope it will either go away or get better by itself. You think you know how the staff member will respond and things are good enough, so why push it? Why? Because the status quo costs you your power, integrity, satisfaction, and your relationships with other staff members, as well as your future. The cost is huge.

Example: "I've been worried to talk to you about something because I think you will react by getting upset. That's not my intention, but I'm worried you'll take it as 'I don't like you' or 'There is something wrong with you' and that's not how I mean it."

STEP 3: *Say it is as though you might be wrong.*
If you say it like you're right, you paint the staff member into a corner. By saying it as though you might be wrong, you give the employee safety and choice — two ingredients necessary for effective communication.

Example: "I could be wrong about this, I could be off, but it looks to me as though you are making a lot of personal calls during business hours."

What goes unsaid in a relationship becomes what the relationship is about. What you complain about is what goes unsaid. Have your own slogan for the next few months. Take a risk. Use my technique outlined above. And "Just Say It."

IGNORED CONCERNS
BECOME BIG ISSUES

It seems like I am always dealing with staff issues. Although I've changed staff members lots of times over my 17 years of practice, tried lots of techniques, read books, even hired two consultants over the last four years to address staff issues, no matter what I try, staff issues always seem to return.

What should I do?

• ◦ •

You have continuous staff issues because you avoid doing something about the concerns that evolve into issues.

Listen closely: *A concern always turns into an issue when you fail to address it.*

The fact is you, like most dentists, avoid addressing staff concerns. You, like other dentists, hope that staff concerns will go away. You hope they'll resolve themselves. But hope is not action. Hope is wishing. As General Patton once said; "Hope is a terrible battle plan." Hope doesn't produce results, action does.

Let me say it another way: A concern left unaddressed always turns into an issue. Issues are much harder to handle than concerns. Issues take much more time and energy to resolve than concerns. So I repeat: Concerns do not disappear by themselves.

What's the difference between a concern and an issue? There is a notable difference in weight, mass, scope, depth and emotion. Concerns and issues have the same core elements: a commitment thwarted, a goal blocked, a value disregarded — or a combination of all three. But invariably, when a concern is left unaddressed, the core elements become much more emotionally charged and greater in volume and weight. When a concern reaches a particular size and weight, it turns into an issue. A molehill becomes a mountain.

Given the heavy cost of leaving concerns unattended, why do dentists continue that behavior? Because they are conflict-averse. They don't want to deal with any concern that might inflame a conflict. So they step over the garbage. And you know what happens to garbage if you don't take it out.

So, get some courage and step into the concerns. Put them on the table. Address them directly. In our Staff Management Program we teach one way to address concerns, but there are hundreds of techniques out there. What's important to remember is if you don't address concerns, they will not go away. They will continue to grow and will soon turn into issues. I can't say strongly enough. Handle concerns ASAP!

Rule of Thumb: "Don't step over the trash. Ever!"

FAIL-SAFE EMPLOYEES

I am a 38-year-old female general dentist. Although I have a staff of just five individuals, I have had high staff turnover ever since I started the practice nine years ago. I'd like to know what I can do to retain staff. Where am I making my mistakes?

. . .

Let's begin with new employees. There isn't anything more risky than bringing a new employee into your practice. After all, the right person can bring new energy and enthusiasm and relieve you of less productive duties, allowing you to concentrate on your grand vision. But the wrong one can irritate other staff members, patients and referrals — in short, do real damage.

What I have found to be the difference between success and failure is what happens during the new employee's first three months on the job. A new book by Harvard Business School Professor Michael Watkins, *The First 90 Days*, fully validates that assertion.

Why are the first three months so crucial? Fellow employees and patients make judgments based on remarkably little data. Those early judgments tend to stick with people. Building credibility in the first three months can propel a new hire through a lot.

But most dentists make very common mistakes with new hires during these first three months. The most common mistake is they don't pay enough attention to the assimilation process. You can't just hire a person and say, "Okay, go!" The person needs to work directly with you to learn the practice — the culture, the politics, "the way it is around here."

Take a look. Is your impulse not to spend time with the new hire, but to leave it up to the rest of your staff or to the departing individual that he or she is to replace? I want you to know this is deadly. It's especially deadly because you, like nearly all dentists, have very strong views about what works and what doesn't. If you don't set out your expectations and values early, you are likely to be very disappointed down the road.

127

I strongly recommend that during the first three months you be really vigilant about trying to spot when new employees are getting into trouble. Usually you can tell by looking in their eyes for that haunted look. And obviously, if they're upsetting the chemistry in your practice there's a problem. You should also look to see if they are moving out of their comfort zone. Or are they immersed in their own functional work only as a means of avoiding the larger issues of working with others and being part of the team? That's the biggest warning sign.

If you see that a new employee is getting into trouble, take action!

Get him or her into your office and see where he or she is struggling. Is it style? Is it resources? Ask how things are going without putting the employee on the defensive. But if he or she is failing and unwilling to talk about it, it's now a matter of managing their exit.

When people start off badly, it is difficult to reverse their direction. If new people make major mistakes and alienate others, they're cooked. If they are merely mediocre, they've still got a shot, but you must nip their counterproductive dynamics in the bud. What usually happens is the new employee does something stupid or wrong and the people around him or her draw back from sharing critical information, which sets the new hire up to make another bad mistake.

A bad hire in a very large practice can be an inconvenience. But for a small practice like yours, it can be a near-death experience. The leverage of an individual in a small practice is huge, which is why small practice owners have to move beyond the sink-or-swim mentality and start directly managing and leading people from the very beginning.

HOW TO PICK WINNERS
AND GET RID OF THE
LOSERS — BEFORE YOU LOSE

Over the last two decades of my practice life I have had many employees. Some I had to fire. Some left because of a change in their situation like babies, husbands relocating, going back to school, changing fields, found another office that would pay more per hour, etc. Only one has stayed for more than eight years. Seems I haven't gotten any better at recognizing and keeping good employees.

How do I recognize a good employee?

• ∘ •

I believe if you "listen" closely to the conversations employees have with you and with each other, you can tell pretty quickly if you have a keeper. In my world-view, "you create yourself in your speaking." The philosopher Heidegger said; "Human beings belong to language." So conversations an employee has with you and other staff is a very clear and accurate diagnostic to what kind of employee she will be.

If you hear "certain" conversations from an employee, she is someone who will contribute rather than distract from the practice. If an employee is engaged in certain conversations, her actions will also be effective and she'll be more of a team player and much more of a commitment in action.

So the coaching is listen for the following good and bad conversations.

Good employees have conversations which include:

1. Asking "What needs to be done?"
2. Asking "What is right for the practice?"
3. Actively listening to you and others.
4. Developing action plans and presenting solutions.
5. Taking responsibility for their actions.
6. Taking responsibility for communicating.

7. Making requests rather than complaining or opining.

8. Focusing on opportunities rather than problems.

9. Thinking and saying "we" rather than "I."

10. Acknowledging and appreciatin2 people around her so as to have the people around her perform better.

Bad employees have conversations such as the following. They:

1. Rarely ask "What needs to be done," but always need to be told what to do.

2. Don't ask "What's good for the practice." They are indifferent to the success of the business.

3. Don't listen to others because they have their own agenda. They usually are a source of gossip. They always push to be right.

4. Don't develop action plans, but blame the problem on someone or something else.

5. Aren't responsible for their actions, but fault, shame or blame others.

6. Don't take responsibility for their communications, but blame others when communication is not working.

7. Complain, opine, gossip rather than make requests.

8. Focus on problems and breakdowns and can't see opportunities.

9. Always come from "I, me and my."

10. Demean, criticize, put-down coworkers so it damages the performance of people around them.

It is common practice to place a new employee on probation for 90 days. She may not master her job duties in 90 days, but during those 90 days she'll have lots of conversations with you and the other employees. If she is engaged in the conversations of "great" employees, she has the potential to be a great employee. If she engages in conversations of a "bad" employee, restart the interview process.

THE FAMOUS 90-DAY
PROBATION PERIOD

Over my 13 years of owning a dental practice, I have always told new employees they are on a 90-day probation period. Given my track record of high staff turnover, I'm wondering what I might do differently during these first 90 days that might dramatically reduce staff turnover?

What I do now is assign someone to be their sponsor, who assists them in their training and goes over the employee handbook with them. Unless it's an assistant, I don't have that much to do with them unless there is a problem later on.

•   •   •

There are two things to consider during those first 90 days of a staff individual's employment. One is what to "look for." Two is what "to do" during these first 90 days.

What I suggest you "look for" in the 90-day probation period is stated very clearly by Jerry Porras, author of *Built to Last* and *Success Built to Last*. He says over and over again; "Don't believe in words, only believe in behavior."

You can tell within the first 90 days if you are witnessing the "real deal" or not. Staff individuals that are high performers will have their walk match their talk. Whether you realize it or not, what you are doing in the first 90 days is judging whether her values and character match her words and actions. In essence you are measuring her integrity by carefully watching to see if her speaking matches her deeds. Do her words line up with her actions?

When the talk doesn't match the walk, then you have someone who is most likely inauthentic, hypocritical or pretending. This sets up a concern about trustworthiness, which by the way is a legitimate concern.

Something else you are looking at is whether her core values line up with your own core values. Core values are so basic, so fundamental, so critical, that if they do not match yours, if they are not in harmony with yours, if she says she embraces your core values but her actions and interactions don't reflect your values, it isn't going to work out — period.

Still another area that you are looking for and evaluating is whether or not she is a team player. If the staff doesn't embrace her in the first month, she will be isolated and ostracized. Some staff will subtly or overtly let you know about their concerns. This is an extremely difficult situation to turn around. Seems once staff makes up their mind, it is hard to change.

That's what you're looking for. At the same time there is also what you do.

What you should be doing in the first 90 days is micro-managing. You should not be "leaving her alone," letting her be trained by the person who is leaving, and hoping for the best. Let me very technical here. When you leave it up to the person who is leaving to train her, then you leave it up to hope it will work out. The management term for this is called "dumb and dumber."

If you want a good employee, you need to invest your time and energy in those first 90 days. Yeah, yeah, I know how busy you are. I know you make your money at the chair. I know you have all those charts to do. I know you have a family. I know all the reasons why you don't have time. Well, how much time have you spent in finding and training new employees given your high turnover rate? How much worry, concern and suffering?

In our consulting and coaching, we strongly recommend that new employees meet with the dentist owner every day for at least two weeks. These don't have to be long meetings. "What's working? What's not working? How are you doing? How's it going with your daily goals?" These are the questions you would be asking.

During those first days, she should have daily goals, targets and objectives. Whatever her job, it should be broken into tiny pieces. An example would be if you hired a new individual to do collections; "Today I request you call eight people in the 30-day column with five direct contacts and four promises for payment." In my consulting lingo it would be you should be making very short term requests, with specific, tangible and measurable outcomes — every day.

132

If she fulfills these requests, then you expand your request from days to weeks and finally to months. By the end of the 90 days, she should have enough of the job mastered that you know the skills are there to get it done.

You see, by making and negotiating requests, she will get what you want, how you want it done and the results she is being asked to produce. And, you'll find out if she can deliver.

Lastly, and most important, you need to be able to pull the switch to let her go if after 90 days you are clear it isn't going to work out. Don't let yourself off the hook, "This is the best I can do. Dental employees are too hard to find. I'm too busy to find another one now." You do far more damage to the practice and actually to this new employee by having her stay and keep on failing at her job because you are too chicken to pull the switch. People, who aren't winning at their job, suffer. Don't let people suffer.

HYGIENE HELL AND BACK AGAIN

I have been in general practice for 21 years. I have had two full-time hygienists for the last nine years. One hygienist has been with me for seven years, the other for five. My issue is keeping my hygiene schedule full. It's a constant battle.

The no-show and cancellation rate always seems too high. The salaries I have to pay the hygienists are simply outrageous and they frequently don't produce enough to cover their expenses. Worse, they often act like prima donnas in the office, refusing to do anything else but their hygiene work. They don't call patients to fill the schedule and forget about helping out at the front desk or cleaning up in the back.

For the money they get paid, I would think they'd care a lot more about the practice than they do. I feel helpless in making this situation better, especially with the shortage of hygienists in my area.

My questions are: How to do I get and keep my hygiene schedule full? And how do I get the hygienists to be team players?

• ◦ •

I hear this same complaint over and over. Let me begin by saying that you probably won't like my answers.

If you're like most dentists, what you want is the magic bullet so you can just get hygiene fixed, so you don't have to worry about hygiene anymore and so you don't have to take any direct action. Sorry, my recommendations won't fix hygiene and I don't have the magic bullet.

There are three steps I suggest you consider taking. None of them is easy. Each requires courage and commitment and each will put you at risk. It is your choice. And as you know, every choice has a consequence. Taking no action and continuing to complain about hygiene is one choice.

STEP 1: This is the hardest part. You need to take full responsibility for your hygiene program. Sorry. You need to stop blaming and faulting your hygienists, the profession, the hygiene schools, your receptionist and your recall patients. You are the owner and head manager of your practice and you are responsible for the performance of your employees, the quality of care they deliver and the level of oral health generated in your practice. You are the bottom line. You are where the buck stops.

Have you forgotten that you are the owner and the one who hired these hygienists? Did it slip your mind that you are the top manager, the one who has the authority to demand and direct action for results? Did you overlook that you are the leader, the one who can generate inspiration, vision, "can do and will do?" It isn't up to them. It is up to you!

I understand how easy it is to cast blame, to fault others, to be the victim and to be resigned. But those are choices you make. They are not the "truth." Things are not written in stone. Why do you make your current choices? You make choices of perception, attitude and relationship so you don't have to be responsible.

So, stop with the "Oh poor me" and "They are doing it to me" and "There's nothing I can do about it." Take full responsibility for your hygiene program and your delivery of hygiene care.

If you can't do that, nothing will change. Can you do that? Better yet, will you do that?

I am willing to bet the farm that you don't hold hygiene as vital, fundamental or critical to the practice. Rather, you hold hygiene as something you need to do, some way to keep on generating restorative for you to do. It is something that patients expect and a way to keep patients around the practice. For you the real action is in your chair as you do your high-end restorative or cosmetic cases. If you could practice without a hygiene department, would you?

The question: Can you shift hygiene from a need to a want?

STEP 2: Generate a new context where hygiene is core to practice success, both clinically and financially. If hygiene for you is just a pain, that's the context of hygiene in your practice. And, as I have said repeatedly, context is decisive.

Let me give you an example of another context for hygiene. Let's say the context is an authentic commitment to continuously improving your patients' oral health. Your current context most likely is maintenance care, or if you're a little fancier, "recare." But what does that context give you? It isn't about improvement. The maintenance context is about maintaining the status quo. It isn't about improving anything. It isn't about making people healthier. In the context of maintenance, your hygiene program has no rousing mission. The current mission, given the maintenance context, is to bring patients back every six months, clean their teeth, push bleaching and get the crown done on 18. Wow, if I was a hygienist, I'd sure be inspired to come to work!

But let's say you declared: "Our hygiene program is committed to improving the oral health of every patient we see." What if you selected some oral health index so you could measure health improvement of your patients over time? What if you said (and really meant it) "The purpose of our hygiene program is to constantly and consistently improve the health of every patient we see!" What if "improving the health of every patient we see" was a true and burning mission of the hygiene portion of the practice? How would hygienists respond to that context? How would patients? Shift the context to one that makes a difference.

STEP 3: Measure and set goals. You need to measure your no-shows and your cancellation rate. You need to set targets. You, not they, need to become a team member of the hygiene team and play full-out to reduce your cancellation numbers. That means you need to talk to your patients about the critical importance of keeping their hygiene appointments. You need to talk about it at their initial exam, and every time you do a hygiene check. You need to be committed to each and every patient keeping the appointments they make. You need to be the team leader in hygiene, not the fuming boss. Those need to be your targets, not theirs.

I know it wasn't the answer you wanted to hear. I suggest you follow Step 1, responsibility, Step 2, context, and Step 3, true targets and see what it gives you. And by the way, if you complete Steps 1, 2 and 3, your hygienists will become team players.

Or you can follow the wisdom of another great philosopher, Yogi Berra, who said, "I never blame myself when I'm not hitting. I just blame the bat. And if it keeps up, I change bats."

STAFF PAY: POLICY OR PAIN!

I am trying to make my office run more like a business. One area where I really struggle is HR. My staff overhead is 34% which I think is too high for a pedo office. But I get bullied into raises at each review. It's not whether or not I will give a raise, it is always a matter of how much.

My staff work extremely hard and I want them paid well, but I don't like the way things are going for evaluations and raises. The staff that are pushier and "enjoy the battle" wind up getting paid more, and the meek and humble get less. So I decided to change the system this year, freeze raises to 2.5 percent cost of living and then at the beginning of each year dole out salary increases all at once and make sure it's closer to 32% of the operating budget.

The concept has not gone over very well with the pushier staff. I feel like the bad guy and am facing mutiny. I can't imagine other businesses operating with a guaranteed raise mentality.

Am I on the right track or is there a better way to get my goals without drawing such a hard line?

. . .

The matter of staff raises nearly always generates discomfort for every dentist in private practice. Staff raises invariably bring tension, upset and anger. The salary transaction promotes resentment and bitterness. Staff salary arbitration becomes a yearly concern causing loss of power and affinity in a dentist's relationship to his or her staff.

It's quite simple. Look at the way you think and act around salary issues (Reread your statement and question.) If you look carefully, you will see the language you use to think about staff salaries has the subject of "I." "I feel, I can't, I decided." This naturally pushes you to "I" versus "them." Not a great place to work from on this issue. A much better approach would be to focus on "what is right for the practice," now and for the future. And if you looked from here, you'd see a whole different world.

From the point of view of "what's right for the practice," you'd notice your lack of a raise policy. Without policy, people govern. When people govern, they are vulnerable to manipulation and domination. When people govern, psychology and personality have the seat of power. So without a raise policy, raises are solely up to you. And of course, the staff figures out ways to squeeze you. Who can blame them, it always works.

It would be far better to sit down with employees and say — "Here is our raise policy. If you want to work in this practice, this is how raises are determined." Then it's not up to you — it's determined by the policy.

What is policy? A policy is a decision that guides, limits or controls many decisions. There are decisions you make, which effect only a specific action at one point in time. That is simply a decision, not policy. A policy is a decision that guides or controls many decisions over a period of time.

Policies need to be written (codified) in order to have power over many decisions over a period of time. The more decisions affected by a policy and the longer the period of time it can be effective, the bigger the policy. Good governance starts with big policies and works to smaller ones as needed.

Examples of *decisions:*

- We will buy this piece of equipment next month.

- We will give Jane a bonus this quarter.

Example of *policies:*
- We will purchase equipment under the following conditions:
    - We have generated the cash to pay for it outright.
    - We will not incur debt to buy equipment.
    - The equipment must be included in our annual equipment budget, or we have decided to substitute a budgeted with an unbudgeted item.

- We will pay staff bonuses once a year on January 31st to all staff on a percentage of compensation bases. The amount available for staff bonuses will not exceed 25% of the practices' before tax profit.

So the objective is to establish policy that governs — governs in such a way that it decides how the practice decides to give raises. We suggest that a raise policy minimally include an annual cost-of-living increase and this be specified in terms of an annual percent increase and what exactly this percentage is based on. Then, additional increases are based on staff performance in four particular quadrants (attitudes/values, behavior/skills, relationships/norms, results/process). How staff is rated and measured in each of these four quadrants is clearly spelled out. How they are scored and how their scores impact their raises is also plainly defined.

As you can tell with these four quadrants, it would take time and consideration, some counsel and benchmarking, to determine how you would calculate performance in each quadrant. But wouldn't it be far more effective to establish a clear raise policy that decides how people get raises rather than you having to decide each and every time?

In my view, what is missing is you do not have a raise policy and without one you will continue to get what you already have — more of the same.

DON'T LOSE WITH LOYALTY

I'm a general dentist in a fairly affluent Colorado suburb. I've been in practice 13 years. I am one of four women dentists in my area. I have five full-time staff and a part-time sterilization assistant. My problem is I have continuously high staff turnover.

For example, over the last year, two of my key staff people, my senior assistant and hygienist, have taken positions with two of my major competitors. It just makes me so angry to have to keep on recruiting and training staff and then lose them.

I think I am a fair and reasonable boss. I think I pay well. I think I take good care of my patients. We have staff meetings. I send my staff to continuing educational programs. We have social events with their families. I have used practice management consultants to work on staff meetings and communication. What more can I do?

It seems I can't find employees that are truly loyal to me or the practice. The exception is I have one employee, my receptionist, who is completely loyal to me. She's been with me for over 10 years. She's never a problem, never argues with me, always supportive. I need four more of 'her.'

How do I get all my employees to be loyal to me and the practice?

• • •

You are not alone. There is a tremendously high turnover rate in dental practices throughout this country. The turnover rate in dental practices is just slightly less than that of fast food restaurants.

Why is there such a high turnover rate in dental practices? There are numbers of reasons and factors. But one major driving force causing this high turnover rate is not the pay, not the lack of opportunity for advancement, not the duties and responsibilities of the job. No, it is the culture within the practice itself.

Most dentists place loyalty right up there with hard work and timeliness on their short list of cherished values. But it's this seeking loyalty from staff that ultimately drives them away.

Dentists want staff who are totally committed to them and their vision. Dentists want staff that will make decisions as if their own money were on the line. Dentists want staff that won't defect to their neighbor down the street. Every dentist wants staff that holds these values as sacred. But are these really the qualities of loyalty?

What dentists really want are "team players" who will implement decisions without any challenge. Dentists want themselves surrounded with "Yes-Women" who will always agree with them. Loyalty to dentists means obedience.

In fact, obedience is an undeclared yet overpowering force in the culture of most dental practices. Look who gets the biggest raises. Look who makes it to the inner circle. And look who is sanctioned with authority in a practice — the "loyal" staff member.

Dentists think it is much easier to get things done when people know their marching orders and debate and disagreement are kept off the table. Staff meetings turn into elaborate agreement sessions. But the costs are far too high. New ideas are never expressed. And all opportunities for real improvement are squashed.

Why do dentists seek obedience? Dentists believe that obedience will produce control, assuming control will reduce stress and anxiety by eliminating conflict, confrontation and disagreement. Dentists fail to realize that *control displaces trust*. The more control requested, the less trust available. So the more obedience demanded by the dentist, the less trust present between the dentist and the staff.

Ultimately a culture of obedience causes good people to leave. You'd be much better off by encouraging thinking and behavior of disloyalty. In this culture, people will tell you what you don't want to hear — the truth about the way things are — like the way you look first thing in the morning without mascara and lip gloss. And being able to have this level of interaction requires trust, not loyalty.

Creating a culture that recognizes the difference between trust and loyalty isn't easy. It requires you to have a thick skin and a tolerance for a certain kind of messiness. But I can tell you that good employees bolt because they are unwilling to work in an obedience culture — not because they are tempted by the offer from the dentist up the block.

It may be time for you to replace the warm light of loyalty with the cold light of truth. It goes both ways. Your staff needs to trust you enough to tell you the truth and be honest with you, and you need to trust them enough to listen.

WHAT YOU DON'T KNOW WILL KILL YOUR PRACTICE!

I don't understand why I can't motivate my staff. They are less than enthusiastic about the practice. It feels like they are only here for the paycheck.

When it comes to team building, you name it, I've tried it. I've done programs on leadership and management. I've hired consultants. We've done team building programs together. I have had bonus systems. Rewards. Trips. But no matter what I try, nothing seems to work. Sure, right after the consultant leaves or we walk out of a program, we perform like a team. But within a month, we're back to the same old stuff.

I've looked everywhere to find the answer. I really want to find out why I can't get my staff to be committed to the success of the practice. I want to know why my staff can't, or won't, perform as a team.

• ◦ •

Do you really want to find out why your staff doesn't respond to you, your leadership or your management? Do you really want to see why they don't hold you in high regard? Do you really want to reveal why they only see their work as a J-O-B? Are you really certain you want to find out?

And what if you do find out? What will do about it? If you do find out, will you confront the issues? If you do reveal the underlying damaging perceptions, will you be willing to change to produce the team you envision?

Most dentists live in a world where ignorance is bliss. It's far easier to blame and fault the staff, dentistry and the world, than to be responsible for creating and maintaining a great staff. In regard to generating a high performance team, it's much easier to criticize them or the circumstances than hold yourself responsible for why the practice has an indifferent staff.

If you look closely, you'll see there is always one constant to not being able to generate a high performance team. There is always one element that is forever present. One factor that is invariable. And that one element is YOU. Yes you! So that's where I'd begin.

Now if you are like most dentists, it's much better not to know how the staff really perceives you so you don't have to deal with what you find out. Let me give you a very clear example. We provide online dental practice management surveys and assessments for our client dentists: Staff Satisfaction, Patient Satisfaction, Dentist Satisfaction, Business Performance, Staff Performance Evaluations, Associate Performance, etc. One of our most powerful survey tools is the Dentist Performance Evaluation.

The Dentist Performance Evaluation is a confidential survey taken by each staff member. The staff, protected by anonymity, assesses the doctor in five fundamental and critical domains: Communication, Leadership, Staff Management, Patient Relations, and Professional Image.

It's straightforward. If the staff perceives the dentist as strong in these domains, then the dentist has a very loyal staff that performs at a very high level. If a dentist has a staff that perceives the dentist as under-performing or failing in any of these areas, the dentist has a staff like yours.

You can find out how the staff sees you and what the staff thinks about you as a leader, manager, practice owner, and clinician. The results of this survey reveal staff perceptions that might undermine your leadership and management. Your job is to confront these perceptions and through communication, commitment and action change these perceptions. Knowing what to work on makes this job very direct; although, it is not always easy or comfortable.

We provide a Report of Findings which explains the results of the survey and contains recommendations for those areas that are under-performing or failing. Additionally, we schedule a 60-90 minute coaching call with a consultant so you can get clear about what the results mean and how to address the staff and make corrections.

Our evidence continues to reveal that improvement in any of these five areas directly impacts staff relations and performance. Improvement in these five areas increases staff loyalty, deepens their commitment and kinship and results in improvement in the bottom line.

This survey has been tested and retested. It is dead-on accurate. Its findings, if addressed by doctor and staff, always produce positive results.

Here are a few sample questions. How do you think your staff would assess you? How do you think your staff would rate you, especially when they know the survey is confidential?

Communicates effectively with all staff members.

Handles conflicts directly.

Consistently provides office leadership.

Does not allow a pecking order.

Has a clear patient philosophy and closely follows it.

Effectively markets the practice.

Works on entire practice having an attractive presentation.

Twenty to thirty percent of each and every dollar you earn goes to the staff. It makes smart business sense that you'd want maximum performance out of this asset. How the staff perceives you as an owner, leader, manager and clinician decides their relationship to you and the practice. Their relationship to you is the greatest determinant in their performance. If you want to find out how your staff perceives you as a practice owner, provider, manager and leader, have your staff take this survey. You'll get your answers point blank.

STAFF WARS

I have a big headache with staff conflicts. I have a staff member who is frustrated that another staff member isn't helping. She also thinks that the other staff member isn't performing her duties. It's a classic case of she said this and she said that. These two staff members have a history of friction. Other staff members have drawn their lines in the sand. "If she quits then I'm quitting," is the phrase of the day. Do I let one go or both?

What do I do?

• • •

Yep, you got a problem. And it's a problem common to many dentists. The bottom line is you need to bring them both in your office and put them at choice.

They can choose 1) to work it out. Or they can choose 2) either one or both of them gets fired. The choice is up to them.

You can only manage people who are responsible. And responsibility begins with choice. Every choice has a consequence. Respond with a "Yes," there's a consequence. Respond with a "No," there's a consequence. Either way there will be a consequence.

Blame and fault are the antithesis of responsibility. So if they are blaming each other, then they are not responsible. When they make it the other person's fault, they are not responsible. When they make the other person wrong, they are not responsible. Responsibility means you hold yourself as "cause" in the matter.

So, if you have to direct, instruct, order or command them in this situation — you put yourself in the position of being responsible. And that may be the way it turns out if they are unwilling to choose. Then you'll need to decide what you want to do; 1) nothing, 2) fire one or 3), fire both.

If they choose to work it out, they'll need to settle their issues. This may require facilitation. You need to be either willing to facilitate their interaction or, if not, get some outside assistance (consultant, mediator or facilitator). However, if you choose to facilitate this interaction — Be Prepared!

First, I suggest you offer them the choice, either Choice One or Choice Two. Let them know if they choose Choice Two, which is to not work it out, one or both will be gone. Not only gone, but gone without references or recommendations and gone without severance pay. Ask them to consider these two options and get back to you in 24 hours.

Next, you need to look at your own responsibility in the matter. You let this go on. You enabled this breakdown by not speaking up and "hoping it would get better on its own." Plain and simple, you chickened out. I'll bet that if you had intervened earlier, it would not have come to this. In fact, I'll bet you recognized this situation weeks or months ago and avoided saying anything. This is your consequence for not speaking up. The cost is high.

The cost is your well being, your future, your power, your production and new patients, your staff morale. What you don't see are the benefits you get from not speaking up when you should have.

The benefits are you didn't need to take a risk, you didn't have to be responsible as a leader and manager, you didn't have to be uncomfortable, you get to be right and make them wrong, you get to avoid being rigorous, demanding and straightforward.

Learn your lesson here and speak up sooner. If you don't, this will happen over and over again.

MOVING STAFF TO HIGH PERFORMANCE

I have finally had enough. I find myself angry with my staff a lot. There are just too many times I see staff members not doing their jobs. I see them goofing off, doing personal stuff, chatting or simply not paying attention. I don't see them fully attentive to patients. I don't see them reaching out to help each other out. I don't see them strongly focused on doing their work.

Staff members appear to be totally focused on themselves and not on the practice. Hygienists are always complaining about pay. Forget that they come in just in the nick of time and leave exactly at 5:00 PM. Assistants seem somewhat indifferent about the quality of their work, having the operatories fully ready or being on time. But in our location, ads for staff can run for weeks, even months. Forget about finding a good employee, just finding an employee is difficult.

I don't know how to tackle this problem. I'm stuffing my anger and not saying anything. But they know I'm upset. I really don't know what else to say to them to turn it around. What are your recommendations?

• • •

Actually the recommendation is straightforward — open your mouth and speak.

What's missing that you can't speak? What's stopping you from communicating to your staff?

What's stopping you is you are afraid to say something. You live in fear. You are immobilized by fear, which restrains you from talking to your staff and making direct and powerful requests.

What are you afraid of?

There are three fears that run you and stop you from communicating. Fear of conflict. Fear of not looking good. And fear of making things worse. Yet without straightforward communication, staff relationships will always become combative and self-centered, results will implode and you will feel isolated.

The solution I suggest is not to be a corrective parent or a domineering boss. Both do more harm than good. Making people wrong only produces a temporary fix. Abuse, intimidation, humiliation and rage never get the job done, nor does fear or bribery work either.

Consultants will tell you, "You need to be assertive. You need to stand up and really express yourself. You must stop being passive." That's not my advice.

When you look, being assertive is about you, and not about them. Being assertive inherently sets up a win-lose or zero sum game. Sure, you feel a lot better about yourself, but it doesn't produce effective action or teamwork in others. So I don't coach people in assertiveness training. Maybe it's a great life-skill, but it's a terrible management practice.

I coach people in what I call "committed communication." A communication model not based on you, but based on them. The goal of the committed communication model is to hold people to their highest selves. To insist that people operate with integrity, demand that people operate as their word and to require people behave ethically, play as a team, and be for others. Committed communication is not for you — it's for your staff and their own self-worth and development.

Committed communication is about seeing people as they want to be, addressing them with dignity and high regard, insisting they operate as their highest selves.

That means you approach staff with respect in a highly ethical manner, in a supportive and encouraging way. You actively listen with empathy. You ask questions that are on point. You ask open-ended questions. You relate respectively, in partnership, insisting on accountability.

If you communicate in this way, staff will behave and deliver in a way that is more consistent with high performance and team. In my world-view, you create yourself and your world in your speaking. How you are thinking, which is speaking to yourself, and how you are talking to the staff, which implicitly tells them they "suck," is producing the outcome you have — a fragmented, self-centered, underperforming staff. It's the old self-fulfilling prophesy.

Don't you yourself want to be addressed as a highly competent and caring professional? Don't you want to be talked to as an intelligent, committed and successful person? Don't you want to operate as you envision your best self? Well, don't you?

Why is staff any different?

So change your lenses and look at staff in a new way. Address them as who they want to be — not who you think they are. You don't need to be assertive or severe. You need to demand they operate consistent with their highest values, vision and commitments — then hold them to these values, vision and commitments. See what that gives you. More importantly, see what it does for them.

The real definition of management is not only getting work done through people, but developing people through work. If staff people have the opportunity to grow, to develop and to attain the ability to operate as their highest selves, you will have a tremendous crew who won't abandon ship.

CAPTAIN JACK & READING THE WAKE

I am never sure how to really evaluate an employee. I sometimes use performance reviews, but that doesn't give me the kind of information I need to make a decision. For example, I have an assistant, Emily, who has been with me for three years. I am not sure if I should keep her or let her go. In some areas she is a decent performer. But in other areas, she doesn't perform nearly as well.

What's a good way to decide whether to keep someone or let them go?

• • •

Years ago I learned about boating. In the late 80s I had a houseboat on Lake Union in Seattle. I also had a 14-foot cruiser with a belligerent in-board out-board motor docked right alongside the houseboat. Being from South Philly, I had zero boating experience and I knew I had to learn something about it.

Down on my dock, there was a seasoned sailor, Jack McFarland, Captain Jack as I came to call him. Captain Jack was in his late 60s, spent his life on boats and totally fit the mold of a cantankerous, weathered sailor. I negotiated a deal with Captain Jack to be my teacher. "Arrr."

Many times, Captain Jack had me sit on the aft of the boat and watch the wake. He also made me watch the wake of other boats. He said you could tell everything about a boat and the way it was being handled by watching the wake. "The wake tells you everything boy. Watch the damn wake!" You could always count on Captain Jack asking; "What does that wake tell you?"

If a boat was going in a straight line, you knew the boat was steadily on course and the captain was paying attention. If it was wavering, you knew something was out of whack. If the boat was sailing smooth and flat, you knew something about the speed of the boat. If the boat was deep in the water, you also could tell about its speed. Captain Jack taught me to read the wake because when you understand the wake, you understand the boat and its captain.

I have found the same to be true of people. As a person works in a practice, she leaves a wake behind her. And just with any wake, there are two sides to a wake that someone leaves behind when moving through a practice. One side of the wake is the job or tasks. The other side is the relationships. When a person travels through a practice for a few months or years, she leaves a "wake" behind in these two areas, tasks and relationship. And you can tell all about the person by the wake she leaves.

In terms of the task, what does Emily's wake look like? Is it a wake of goals being reached? Is it a wake of complete work? Is she directly contributing to the mission being fulfilled? Is she figuring out the best way of doing things? Is she making what she does better than it was before?

Or is there a different kind of wake?

Are goals not achieved? Are there continual misfires? Is the mission not accomplished? Is there a lack of completion? Is there disorganization and chaos? Inactivity? Nothing happening? Lack of focus? False starts? Resources and money lost?

You can tell from the wake the level of performance and results. In practice, results matter. They are the stuff on which you evaluate your staff. Results are what bring your vision into reality. At the end of the day, what kind of results from her tasks did she leave behind her? The wake is the record she leaves behind her.

On the other side of the wake are the relationships. Just as she leaves the effects of her work behind her in results, she leaves the effect of her interactions with people behind in their hearts, minds and spirit. She leaves a wake as she moves through the lives of her coworkers. She leaves a wake as she moves through the lives of patients. And she leaves a wake as she touches your life. What does that wake look like?

Are people uplifted, smiling and having a great time as she moves through their lives? Are they better off or worse off? Do they consider her a blessing or a curse? What is the nature of her wake? Are coworkers and patients smiling or reeling? Does her relationship enhance others' performance or take away from their performance?

So check out Emily's wake and decide. The wake tells you all you need to know. Aye matey, might be time to have Emily walk the plank!

GETTING STAFF TO DO
THE RIGHT THINGS

I've been in practice four and half years. I'm not doing as well as I thought I would be at this stage of practice. I'm basically just getting by. One major problem is the same issues keep on recurring with my staff: personal phone calls, lateness, gossip, back-stabbing, weak performance, indifference, blame and complaining. I'm at my wits end.

I've fired and hired some new people, but that doesn't seem to change anything. Initially it seems to work, but after a short while, it's back to the way it has always been.

How do I get my staff to do the right things?

• • •

In my years of consulting, I have witnessed a great number of dentists generating miraculous results. According to the dictionary, a miracle is an event in reality beyond and out of the ordinary. My observation is these miraculous results are not genetic but environmental. What I have found is the secret to a great practice is great staff performance and great staff performance is a result of "alignment."

Alignment requires you remove from your practice all the stuff that is inconsistent with your vision, your passion and your goals. And by the way, that includes people. Sounds harsh. Sorry, I can't help that. It is the way it is.

Bottom Line: You bring into your practice everything that supports who you are and what you want to create. Choose wisely. But remember, this is a process, not a light switch. It's tough and it takes time.

Your actions, intention and attention should be paid to generating and maintaining alignment. There are lots of ways to build alignment. Some dentists hire consultants like me to assist them in building alignment. Others use CE programs, books, software, study clubs and the Internet. But no matter what model or method you use, building alignment is the one element always present in highly successful practices.

Pick a behavior you don't like going on in your practice, one that you'd like to get rid of, one that just keeps showing up again and again. Look and list everything in your practice environment that rewards and promotes this behavior. This includes "your" actions as a leader and a manager toward this behavior. Now list all the things that would block or thwart this behavior. My bet, and I haven't lost this bet in 20 years, you'll find the first list a lot longer than the second list.

Now, pick a behavior you like, something that's really important for practice success that isn't happening enough. Do the same analysis. You'll invariably find the list of things blocking that behavior a lot longer than the list of things that promote that behavior.

You see, it's all about the payoffs. You are unconsciously reinforcing or sabotaging staff behaviors and making it much harder to achieve your goals. The trick is to get your message and your incentives aligned with the behaviors you really want.

Here's an example. I have few orthodontist-clients in Oregon and Nevada that love to play golf. When I ask them why they play golf, they tell me they play the game for peace of mind, to relax, to be with nature, to hang out with friends, to be themselves, to let go. But these guys take lessons. When I talk to the pro who gives some of them their lessons, and ask the same question, the pro tells me they say things like stop my slice, fix my short game, improve my score, get me more power — all the things that golfers want.

Their first answer has to do with enjoyment. The second answer focuses on what is wrong with their game. In golf as in dental practice, there is a problem when goals are not aligned with meaning. There is pretense. There is hypocrisy. There is a real disconnect between speaking and action, which reveals a lack of integrity.

I understand it takes tremendous commitment, discipline and courage to continuously engage in generating alignment. It's so much easier to sell out and just accept the easy, safe, non-threatening, avoid-conflict routine. But as a business owner, as a leader and as an executive manager, your job, your accountability as an owner is to align meaning, thinking and action.

You need to really understand what I'm saying here. You need to understand this challenge of keeping things aligned never ends — never. But if you want success, if you want high performance from your staff, you better suck it up and get your team aligned. And don't be afraid to show them the door if they're not buying in.

It's really very simple in my view. When the integrity is in, miraculous results get produced. Integrity occurs when what you say, what you mean, and how you act are totally aligned. So my coaching is become demanding, arduous, unrelenting about integrity in your office. But that must include rigorously holding yourself to your word — no matter what. If you can do this, if you can sustain this discipline, if you don't waver, I can promise you the results in staff performance.

LIAR, LIAR, PRACTICE ON FIRE

I find myself unable to be honest with my staff. I have it clear in my head what I want to say, but I never do. When I talk to the staff, either individually or at staff meetings, I am not really straight or direct with them. I understate, mollify and lie. When I do this, I feel terrible about myself.

Why do I lie to my staff? Why can't I just be brutally honest?

• • •

It's pretty clear why we lie. We lie because of fear. We lie as a solution to our fear, our fear of how somebody will react to a truth we may tell them. We lie because we are afraid we will have to cope with someone's negative or emotional reaction to us. We lie because we're afraid we'll cause an upset and incur the disturbing reactions that come with it.

The payoff of lying is clear. We lie because it's safer. We lie so as to reduce the risk. We lie to keep the status-quo the status-quo, because we at least know what the status quo is. We lie to get us off the hook. We lie so we can avoid being held to account to our commitments as an owner. We lie because it is politically correct and won't put us in any form of jeopardy. We lie so we can blame others and not be responsible ourselves. We lie because it's easier than telling the truth.

But you and I know the cost of lying. It costs us our integrity. It costs us our self-worth. It costs us our power. It costs us our well being. It costs us our relationship with that person and without a relationship in place, it costs us any future with that person.

If you want an employee who isn't lied to in your relationship, then she'd better be a person who can respond and not react to unwelcome news. But the same holds true for you. That means from the very beginning of your relationship, from the moment she sits down across the desk for the interview, you tell her the truth. And she needs to know that it's safe to tell you the truth. In this way, you establish a reality in your staff member's experience that it is productive rather than destructive to be honest with each other.

As the leader, manager and owner of your practice, you need to get through your fear about your staff's reaction to your truths. You need to have courage and be willing to step into all sorts of fears — they may not like you, they might find it upsetting, they may judge you, they may quit, they may think you are a terrible person.

Believe me, I appreciate that you are afraid your staff will withdraw their affection, their kinship, their affinity, their support and commitment. I appreciate these fears may, in fact, be based on past real experiences. But so what! The costs are far too high not to be straight with your staff. Is it really worth it not to take the risk?

As difficult as it may seem, you need to tell the truth. It's the only thing that will work in the long run. Lying may give you what you want in the short run — safety, being left alone, the status-quo, but lying is simply reactive and never ultimately satisfying. You need to have the courage to stop going for safety and comfort and go instead for what will work. Telling the truth will get you long term satisfaction and significantly enhance your power.

Every time you lie, you reinforce the thoughts, attitudes, beliefs and feelings about the other person and yourself (who you consider yourself to be that has to lie). So my coaching is make a list of the people you lied to in your practice. Sit them down, and tell them the truth (If you want a little coaching on how to ignite the process of truth-telling, e-mail me. We have trained hundreds of dentists in "how to say the hard things to staff.")

Any act of avoidance of a fear reinforces the fear. Any time you act out of fear, it keeps the fear alive. When you lie out of fear, your fear persists. Is that the way you want to be with your staff? Afraid? Is that the way you want to be in your practice?

Give yourself the biggest gift possible for New Years. Give yourself the gift of the truth. My promise is if you have the guts to do this, your integrity and power will be restored and you will be much more effective in leading, in owning and in managing your practice as a successful business.

As Mark Twain is quoted as saying; "Courage is resistance of fear, mastery of fear, not the absence of fear." It is always, and I mean always, an existential leap of courage to open your mouth and speak the truth. But that courage is often the difference between a highly successful practice-owner and one who is not.

POWER STARTS WITH CLARITY

I've always had problems with my staff. High turnover, poor performance, and lack of team spirit are characteristic. Now, it's worse than ever with bickering, gossip and back-stabbing. The front and the back are at war. How do I get my staff to change their behavior and attitude so I don't have these problems?

• ○ •

When problems are seemingly intractable and you are confused and struggling to resolve them, I suggest you address your problems by generating "clarity."

Clarity is having a specific image about what you want. When most dentists have a problem, all they know is what they don't want. And they may only have a vague idea of what they do want.

If I ask you, "What is it you want?" and that you describe it in vivid detail, how would you respond? Would your description of "what you want" be tangible, clear, specific? Would your answer explain to me exactly how what you want would be measured? Would your response tell me in precise fashion, how it would feel when you got what you want?

Most likely not!

More than likely you'd respond in vague generalities, which means you have no idea what you want. All you have is a very specific image of what you don't want. You don't realize that holding images of what you don't want renders you powerless.

I'll bet you spend most of your time trying to manage or eliminate what you don't want. No power can exist in this context. Even if you liberate yourself of what you don't want, you will still be without what you do want since you have no idea what that is.

In your case, you want a staff that doesn't fight, doesn't back-stab, and gets along. You are upset with the front and back being divided and bickering. You probably feel your patients are being mishandled because of this rift. That's what you don't want. What do you want?

Here's another example. A senior doc has an associateship that isn't working. He brought on the associate based on what he didn't want. He didn't want to be on call 24/7. He didn't want to be under so much stress given the business of his practice. He didn't want the pressure of not being able to see a new patient for 6 to 8 weeks. He didn't want the strain of managing the staff himself. He didn't want the burden of ownership, making all the decisions by himself. He brought on an associate based on what he didn't want. He never thought about what he wanted. He wasn't clear on the future he wanted to have emerge, only those things he didn't want in his future. It's no wonder most associateships fail.

Clarity is about what you want. All my clients who get what they want start with generating a clear picture of what it is exactly they want. The kind of power my clients seek is the power that serves rather than abuses, and this kind of power requires clarity.

Let's try this exercise. Take a chronic, unresolved problem and rather than telling me what you don't want, describe to me precisely what you do want.

> *What would it look like if your staff were a high performance team?*
> *How would they communicate with each other?*
> *How would they support each other?*
> *What would their accountabilities look like?*
> *How would you measure their performance?*

You see what I'm getting at? You haven't a clue what it would look like, you only know what you don't want it to look like.

One thing about a good business coach is he or she would work with you so that you could fully and clearly articulate what you want. Sure you'd begin with what you don't want. But you can't have it unless you can see it clearly, once you can envision it, once you can clearly visualize it.

It's just like your dentistry. If you can't clearly envision the final result after your diagnosis, you can't make a compelling offer to the patient. Without clarity you have no power, so they most likely will not accept your treatment recommendations. Same on the business side of the house. No clarity, no power.

YOU DON'T NEED TO MOTIVATE A MOTIVATED STAFF

I have always had difficulty motivating my staff. What are the keys to making it happen?

• ◦ •

There are libraries of books, reams of articles, endless DVDs and CDs, Podcasts and streaming video about motivating staff. But if you really want to understand how great practices crack this code, you need to look much deeper. My particular view about how to produce and maintain a highly motivated staff resides in the relationship between the staff and the practice.

You can't have motivation without a special relationship existing between the staff and the practice. Simply put, the staff has to love the practice.

Staff loves a practice when they feel valued, acknowledged, appreciated and known. When the staff can see a future in which they themselves have real opportunities to grow and develop. When they feel great about what they do, whom they do it with and where they're going. Then, they love the practice. If any of these elements are missing, you'll never (and I mean never ever) motivate your staff.

Everything else that makes a practice extraordinary — leading edge dental services incorporating the latest technologies, fabulous relations with vendors and suppliers, a whiz-bang Website, outstanding clinical gurus and mentors, digital radiography, flat screen monitors in every operatory, Italian décor throughout, mood lighting, outstanding business advisers and consultants, well tested business systems and structures, solid policies and procedures, state-of-the-art computing systems, warm scented facial washcloths — doesn't count. Success always comes down to who does the work of the practice, day in and day out and that's the staff. What makes a practice great is a great staff.

Now I'm speaking about more than "happy" employees. There are plenty of happy staff members in practices that don't have this kind of mojo.

It isn't just about the compensation, perks and benefits, as important as they might be. There's something else shaping the work environment, something that promotes a profound sense of belonging. Staff feels a kind of psychic ownership of the practice.

Staff doesn't just work here, they *belong* here. They feel a deep sense of responsibility for the success and future of the practice. As I work with clients, if staff doesn't have this relationship with the practice, the practice will never be great and the staff will never be motivated — no matter how many bonus systems you throw at them or all-expense-paid trips you promise.

Several key elements create this kind of ownership relationship. One, the staff never doubts that the practice, the dentist, and the other staff members care about them personally. Each staff person knows that the dentist and the other staff members will stand by them through thick and thin as long as they hold up their end of the bargain.

Second is integrity. If you fail to honor yourself as your word, if you don't do everything you can to keep your promises, if you are at all hypocritical and pretentious, staff will not trust you. No trust, no unconditional commitment. No unconditional commitment, no sense of wanting to be responsible. You must, at all times, walk the talk.

Last, articulating, constantly demonstrating and being a dental practice with a higher purpose. A purpose that is constantly reflected in the kind of work the practice does, the way the practice does its business, and the recognizable good it provides from delivering its dentistry. No matter how the higher purpose is framed, it serves the same function — it makes the work of staff meaningful, it makes them feel that their contribution matters and it motivates them to give their best effort.

In great practices, the higher purpose is a constant expression. It is not a mission statement that is talked about once a year or a vision statement you run up the flagpole at annual meetings. The higher purpose is a thread that is woven into the fabric of the practice and shows up in how it operates each and every day. The higher purpose is a constant presence which people never lose sight of and never forget about.

If you can create this kind of environment in your practice, you will have a practice where staff knows they are interrelated and in charge and no one is looking over their shoulder. Where the staff knows everyone is counting on them. Where staff feels trusted and knows that if they run up against a problem, they are safe to talk about it because they are part of a *higher purpose.*

If you can create this kind of environment in your practice, then you don't need to motivate staff because the staff will already be motivated.

YOU GET WHAT YOU ASK FOR

Over my 11 years in practice, I have never had a staff that does things right. I've hired consultants, facilitators, communication specialists, psychologists, taken courses, fired, hired — you name it, I tried it. I just can't seem to get the staff to do the right things. In fact, most of the time I find myself correcting them because they did it wrong.

I'm tired of my staff not doing things right. I'm tired of having to micromanage them. I'm upset that I can't find good people who want to do their job right.

What do I need to do get my staff to perform like winners, not losers? I know if I had a good staff my revenue would be much higher, I'd have more new patients and I'd have a lot fewer headaches.

•   ◦   •

The universe always gives you what you ask for. So when you make the staff wrong, the universe gives you what you ask for — a staff that does things wrong.

The universe responds by providing a fitting response to your declaration. The universe consistently answers back; "Hey, you want a staff that does things wrong, no problem. I can handle that. I'll make sure the staff does stuff so they are wrong. Here you go."

Making your staff wrong for their behavior bolsters and boosts what they do that you see as wrong. Making them wrong keeps them and you stuck, diminishes effective action and weakens the staff's ability to produce results. But remember, you're getting exactly what you are asking for.

Why do you do it? Why do you make the staff wrong? First and foremost, making the staff wrong makes you right. People would rather be right than happy. You would rather be right than change. Making your staff wrong takes you off the hook because you can blame them and fault them. You can make them responsible. You can be the victim.

In your situation, by making the staff wrong, you are making them responsible for the poor performance and outcomes of your practice. The staff is your reason for why your results stink. They are the cause of the lack of new patients. Meanwhile you get to be the poor little powerless good guy.

Making your staff wrong diminishes your power since it expands your view that you cannot do anything to enable and empower your staff. In other words, making your staff wrong diminishes you, reduces your capacity to do something about it. Ultimately, it devalues who you are. It squeezes down your self-esteem.

Making your staff wrong extracts leadership from your being. Leaders speak a future that's possible, a future that will make a difference. Yes, they want to right a wrong, but they define the wrong so they can dedicate themselves to making it right. They don't define the wrong so they can make themselves right.

You wouldn't like me as your coach in the least. I wouldn't let you get away with this thinking and behavior. Your staff doesn't need to be fixed — you do!

By your thinking and actions, the staff does things you see as wrong. They have no other choice. You know the "reap what you sow" business. First you must understand you are cause in the matter. You are the one making this happen. You are the one that has them doing things to be wrong so you can be right. That's your first step. Take responsibility for the way the staff performs. A good coach doesn't blame his players when the team loses. He takes responsibility for how the team played.

Once you assume responsibility, then there are numbers of action steps possible that would change staff behavior and performance. But no change is possible without a change in you. And the change begins with you: accept responsibility and stop making them wrong. If you can't do that, no matter what you do, what you try, who you hire to "fix them," it will always fail.

WRONG, WRONG, WRONG

I was really upset last week when my hygienist left an hour early. She left when she found out her last patient cancelled without letting me or my assistant know. She just announced it to the front desk and left.

We were having one of those crazy days. When she left I still had two emergencies sitting nervously in the waiting room, 30 minutes behind and I had one front desk out sick. How could she just leave and not help out? I really got angry.

When she came in the next day I "blasted" her. She has been sullen and repressed ever since. Now I'm worried she's going to quit.

What else could I have done?

• ○ •

You made her "bad" and "wrong." When you make someone bad and wrong, they invariably justify why they took the action they did — since they don't want to be bad and wrong.

When you make someone wrong, they respond by resisting being responsible. When you make someone wrong, they unconsciously blame you for why they did what they did. "He's such a jerk," or "The rest of the staff doesn't appreciate me."

When you make someone wrong, there are always consequences — even though they ARE wrong. Making someone wrong doesn't work. Making someone wrong always results in a situation where they will not be responsible, they will turn around and make you wrong, and they will blame you for why they did what they did. So as a manager, when you make someone wrong, you make matters worse not better. You may feel better at the moment because you "got it off your chest," but it doesn't produce the outcome you are looking for.

Before you blast a staff member, before you make them bad and wrong, let me recommend a model of communication that works. I suggest you use this model to produce results and move them to take appropriate action.

Open with your own statement of responsibility. In other words, take responsibility for her poor performance. *I'm not sure what I am doing wrong as a leader and manager, but whatever it is, it's not working. I'm just not getting the job done with you in that you didn't realize leaving early doesn't work.*

By taking responsibility yourself, you allow them the space to take responsibility for themselves. You can't manage people who are not responsible. It all begins with responsibility. When you make them wrong, when you try to make them feel bad by using guilt, when you blame them, when you fault them, you invariable extract responsibility not expand it.

Next, ask her what you can do as a manager and leader to have her see that staying and assisting others is what you want to communicate. *What am I not doing as a leader and manager, what am I not saying, that would instill this kind of team perspective in you?*

Again, you are standing in responsibility. You are not blaming or faulting her. You are not applying guilt. You are not making her wrong. By asking the question, she is now going to look from responsibility — you're shifting where she is standing.

After she answers your question, repeat her answer so she knows she's been heard. Then ask her "what happened" that she didn't realize or didn't recognize the need to stay around and help out." Listen. Again, repeat back what you heard them say.

Now ask her for a declaration, promise or request.

You see if you can move people to first be responsible and then have them make legitimate commitments, you'll get your job done as a manager.

MAKING IT REAL

I have regular staff meetings and I always have a morning huddle. We go over the numbers. We set goals and targets. We review the operations and what needs to be corrected to make things work better. However, these meetings rarely produce the outcomes and results I want. Why?

• ∘ •

Much of my work is about coaching people to speak in a way that makes a difference. The way you and many dentists speak about what is going on in the practice leaves the staff indifferent, apathetic, and unresponsive. You report activities or numbers in a way that leaves your staff uninspired. If you're going to speak to your staff, formulate your speaking in a way that makes an impact.

In Stephen Covey's book, *The 8th Habit*, he describes a poll of 23,000 employees drawn from a number of companies and industries. He reports the poll's findings:

- Only 37 percent said they have a clear understanding of what their organization is trying to achieve and why.

- Only one in five was enthusiastic about their team's and organization's goals.

- Only one in five said they had a clear "line of sight" between their tasks and their team's organization's goals.

- Only 15 percent felt their organization fully enables them to execute key goals.

- Only 20 percent fully trusted the organization they work for.

This is pretty sobering. It's also very abstract. After you read this information, you may walk away thinking, "There's a lot of dissatisfaction and confusion in these companies." But the way it is reported, the way it is spoken, generates no real emotional impact. There is no call to action. There is no wonderment about what can be done to change it. Likely there is just a sense of discouragement and resignation, and in a few minutes all of these stats will soon be forgotten.

Covey follows these statistics and superimposes a human metaphor over them: "Let's say a soccer team had these same scores. Only 4 in 11 of their players on the field would know which goal is theirs. Only 2 of 11 would care. Only 2 out of 11 would know what position they play and know exactly what they are supposed to do. And all but two players, in some way, would be competing against their own team rather than the opponent."

I'll say it again: Context is decisive. By shifting the context from statistical analysis to a human condition, you hear the same information in a totally different way. And that's what you need to figure out how to do it (speak it) when you report to your staff. Speak it in a way that gives it a "human context."

Staff cannot connect to numbers alone. You need to connect the numbers, the stats, or the underperforming activities to match or touch something human so they can embrace what you are saying.

Whether you're talking to staff or patients, begin to speak in a way that really hits home. "You have extensive distal caries on number 30 that should be addressed immediately or you might need a root canal."

Or "You have a large cavity on the back of your first molar that if left untreated will most likely cost you the tooth?" Which one grabs you?

"Your job description is clear on room set up, tray set up and seating patients. Please follow the protocol."

Or "Keeping patients waiting makes them apprehensive and more nervous than they already are. Every minute we're late raises their anxiety level another notch." Which one will most likely move the assistant to action?

The more your can deliver your speaking to fit experiences that people have, the more they will hear what you have to say. As an exercise this week, try to design "human" conversations around your numbers and deliver it that way to the staff and see what that gives you.

CONTEXT OF
MARKETING

MARKETING is a conversation, a conversation that happens outside the walls of the practice. A marketing conversation can either be passive or active. Passive marketing conversations include brochures, radio spots and ads.

Passive MARKETING attempts to lure new patients to the practice like a net cast out to entrap fish. It is generalized in scope, typically expensive and usually produces a very small return on investment.

Because it is passive, using representative materials or media, there is little risk required. No direct interaction is needed between the dentist and others. Safe. Just put it out there and hope it draws in a few new patients.

The active MARKETING conversation has proven time and again to produce far better results while infusing an atmosphere of excellence and expectation in the practice. When an existing patient speaks to a neighbor, friend or colleague, it is a conversation based on trust and contribution. When a practice is soliciting through letters or ads or radio spots, it is a conversation of coercion or seduction. A communication coming from someone you know and trust has a great deal more power than a communication coming from a dentist through printed materials or other forms of media.

Our model of MARKETING is about generating active marketing conversations. It is creating a practice culture that truly understands why patients should be referring friends and family. It is a practice that can stand for "We provide the best care possible with the greatest attention to service and concern for patients' health and well being." The conversation doesn't market the physical walls of the practice or the coolest technologies. It markets excellence, satisfaction and value. Patients in that consumer situation, experiencing excellence, satisfaction and value will market the practice to their friends, family and peers if guided directly by the dentist and staff.

DELIVERING EXCEPTIONAL SERVICE

I really enjoyed the newsletter on service. My question is how do I get my staff primed and committed to delivering the kind of service you wrote about?

In terms of my practice management, I feel I am doing well. I've established a strong infrastructure, better-than-average operational efficiencies, clear goals based on reality and a functional budget. I have a production plan that we rigorously follow and meet over 95% of the time.

I have some reasonably good marketing efforts in play. I've developed a very attractive office. I have a great location. And compared to many dentists, I'm doing quite well. But I know that we could do better and I believe this improvement is in the area of service.

My staff does their jobs pretty well, they get along fine with each other, but other than that they seem to be focused quite a bit on themselves; getting out on time, making more money and protecting their turf. It's not that they're not gracious with patients, but it isn't the level of service that I know is possible.

I don't see a clear path on how to get my staff focused and delivering exceptional service.

• ∘ •

There is nothing like experience to make the point about service. Find two similar enterprises, one that provides great service, another that doesn't, and then send staff members on their own to both places. Have them shop or eat and then report their experience.

You see, most dental practices have access to the same materials, techniques, information, consultants, training, perks, benefits, and pay range for staff. So why do some staffs soar while others flounder at providing great service? The difference cannot be in these "things" — the functions, processes and structures — since they are basically available for every dental practice.

So what is it that brings out a staff's commitment to service? Patients don't have a relationship with a practice, they have a relationship with the people in the practice. The formula is straightforward: The higher the level of service from the staff equates to increasingly greater depth and loyalty of the patient to the practice.

Now the question becomes: *What's the source of staff wanting to be of service to your patients?* The answer is passion. A passion for service is the source of great service.

A passionate staff that constantly shows their commitment to people will engender patients' loyalty, greater acceptance of treatment, better compliance with oral hygiene and post-op care, and they will refer others. It is your job as the leader in your practice to incite and sustain passion in your staff. The passion has to come from you first. You're the generator. As a leader, you must be passionate about service. If you're not, you're staff never will.

Passion is tremendously powerful. Most dentists are very passionate about their dentistry. They fervently care about their work. They are obsessive about the quality of dentistry they deliver. They are clearly zealous and devoted to what they do and how they do it. This passion might explain why the clinical CE industry is a multi-billion dollar industry. This passion might explain why the guru's of restorative dentistry are pulling in $8K for a weekend course, having dentists waiting in line to get in. This passion might explain why dental suppliers have double digit margins since dentists are eager to purchase the latest and greatest. Passion is a powerful driving force.

But is there the same level of passion present in dental practice for really taking care of people, for serving people? If you have an authentic passion for taking care of people at the highest level, combined with a passion for your dentistry, then you have all you need to have the staff be passionate about their work and fully serve your patients.

The higher the level of passion for something, the more intolerant, protective, demanding, driven, empowered and focused you are on that thing. You'd fire someone for hurting your ability to produce clinical excellence. But would you be willing to fire someone who harmed or thwarted superior patient service?

My suggestion is that you first check your passion for really taking extraordinary care of people. If that is missing, find out why! As I said, without you being passionate about "customer service," you're staff never will be.

MARKETING 101

I am working on selecting a consultant for marketing. Both consultants I am considering recommend multicolor brochures, Websites, new logo, name change, new stationery, redoing the waiting room, etc. Each one is really expensive. I could easily spend $30,000 to $50,000. How do I make the right decision?

Can you give me some advice?

. o •

The advice I am going to give you is the opposite of what your consultants are recommending.

Read the following very carefully and take it to heart. It is accurate. We teach this in our Mastery program. This information is valid for general dentists as well as specialists.

First, there are, in reality, five kinds of marketing activities in dental practice: 1) broadcasting, 2) courting, 3) superpleasing, 4) nurturing and 5) listening.

Broadcasting includes all those activities that generate leads or inquiries to new patients or new referrals. Broadcast activities include brochures, stationary, seminars, books, articles, newsletters, Websites, presentations and study clubs. You have more than one person in the audience. You do not have a professional relationship with them. You are explicitly or implicitly broadcasting a message in hopes of generating inquiries, contacts or requests from people to be patients of your practice or, if you are specialist, to refer to your practice.

Broadcasting is usually an outsourced service. The outsourced companies, the consultants and vendors, want to sell you a bucketful of broadcast stuff — their time, brochures, logo, stationery, Websites, etc. And because dentists are extremely gullible, they buy a lot of that stuff. Unfortunately for them, broadcasting is by far the weakest and least-productive of any marketing activity.

If you are lucky enough to get a response from broadcasting you go a-courting. You develop a kind of courtship routine in hopes of pushing the relationship to one where the potential patient chooses you. That might be a phone call or a personal letter. You try to make the person feel special and that you are the one and only dentist he or she should be seeing. Courting also costs a lot of time and money. And because it is a byproduct of broadcasting, it doesn't produce very good results.

So, these two activities, broadcasting and courting, produce the fewest results. That's right. They have the smallest ROI and cost the most money and time. But you'll have multicolor brochures and a Flash program on your Website. How very cool. Be aware, like the sirens were to Ulysses, so are brochures and Websites to dentists. Strap yourself to the mast or you will certainly be seduced.

The old adage that there is no more effective marketing than word of mouth is valid in dentistry. To enhance word of mouth, I recommend you superplease, nurture and really listen to existing patients — or referrals — on existing matters. That means much more than doing outstanding technical work. You need to service your patients or referring dentists so they are far more than just satisfied, they are delighted.

My recommendation is that you invest your time and money on superpleasing, nurturing and really listening to your current patients or referring docs. Be willing to spend more time with them off the clock, discussing future issues and concerns. The more time you spend on those activities — superpleasing, nurturing, and really listening — the better your marketing will be. That is what creates word of mouth.

Look at your colleagues who have spent $8,000 on brochures, $10,000 on Websites, $7,000 on logo design and stationery and $15,000 on study clubs. Then add the time they spent on getting those things up and running and the time they now spend maintaining them. You can double or triple the cash outlays to come to the total cost. Now look at their ROI. I can promise you, if they had spent their time superpleasing, nurturing and listening, they would have done a whole lot better in generating new patients and saved themselves a ton of money and time.

So, if you want my advice, keep your money in your pocket and take fabulous care of your patients. It's as simple as that.

SUPERPLEASING

I want to "superplease" my patients, but I can't get the staff focused on it. They pay more attention to getting to work just in the nick of time, leaving on time and getting their own jobs done. They've all been with me a long time, get their jobs done and, really, they are pretty efficient. It's not that they aren't nice to patients or polite, but they certainly don't go above and beyond to really make patients feel special.

What should I do?

• • •

Good question. The answer is not one you will like, but I promise it is the right answer to your question. It is much less about your staff and much more about you.

I believe you have not taken a stand that patients will be superpleased in your practice. You are not a demand that each and every patient be superbly taken care of. You probably tolerate patients being treated as objects. Yes, I know they are treated nicely and politely, but still your staff sees them as objects to be moved around so they can get their jobs done and get out on time. Putting patients first so they are unexpectedly delighted because you far exceeded their expectations is not Job One. In fact, it's not even on the job chart.

Furthermore, I suspect you are totally resigned to the situation because you have settled for good enough is good enough. You think, "Because the staff isn't causing trouble, why make trouble by making demands? They get their jobs done. Why make waves?"

Why, indeed! Your ability to attract and sustain great new patients depends on exceeding your patients' expectations so that their experience in the practice is memorable. And when a patient's experience is memorable, he or she shares that experience with others, generating new patients.

You have a severe case of WPI, better known as "wimp-puppy-itis." Symptoms of "wimp-puppy-itis" are seen in staff members' indifference to team play, their lack of *superpleasing* patients, their leaving exactly at 5:00 PM no matter what and their only doing what they have to do.

Symptoms seen in dentists include avoiding conflict or confrontation with staff members by hiding in their private offices, pretending to be busy, being hypocritical and acting as if everything is fine, being nice to staff members in order to avoid any conflict by placing demands or making few if any strong requests and hoping the staff will get better on its own.

My Rx: Take a stand about the way you want patients treated in your office and don't back down.

REFERRALS: HERE TODAY, GONE TOMORROW

I read your missives on Word of Mouth marketing a while back. My staff and I began to follow your recommendations and actively ask patients to refer new patients. It took us a month and several staff meetings to get us to where we could ask about half our patients a day to refer, but we did it.

Within 90 days, our number of new patients increased by 50 percent. We went from 12 new patients to 18 new patients a month. Asking patients to refer was really working. But now, six months later, no one is asking for new patients anymore, including myself. Now I am back to 11 to 12 new patients a month and we need to begin the process all over again. I was thinking about using a bonus system to reignite our asking for referrals.

Why didn't we sustain this effort, especially when we all saw it working?

• ⁕ •

Most likely some emergency initiated your effort around new patients. In your case, my guess is the instigator was a protracted lack of new patients, which led to a lack of production, resulting in cash flow problems. Then, once your emergency had passed, the driving force to sustain the initiative disappeared.

As I have said many times, I don't recommend using a bonus to motivate staff to keep asking patients to refer new patients. I am not a big fan of bonuses because they inherently use a carrot and stick approach to generate actions that staff should be doing anyway. Furthermore, in my experience, bonuses eventually lead to more trouble than the problem they solved.

So then, how do you get staff to "want to" ask patients to refer if you can't use the stimulus of bonuses? There are two concurrent approaches — one is through management and the other through leadership.

Part of management's job is not only to produce results through people, but also to develop people through work. Asking patients to refer is a powerful way to develop people through work. Sure, the staff can see the value for you as the dentist and owner in having them ask for referrals. You get more new patients; you are busier, making more money, feeling validated and useful, and you're less stressed. But in this view, staff may not see the value for themselves.

If the staff were to see personal value from asking patients to refer new patients, they would be empowered to continue. But on the surface, asking patients to refer is risky business. There is always the underlying fear of rejection, appearing unprofessional or coming across as a salesman. But if they recognized the real and immediate value from asking patients, they might be more willing to take the risk and overcome these barriers.

What value can staff members derive from asking patients to refer new patients? Increased self-worth and confidence in conquering their fear of making requests; validation that they work in a dental practice that provides exceptional service; enhanced team camaraderie that arises from sharing risk; increased confidence in you as a dental provider.

The second element is a function of leadership. As a leader, you want to inspire staff to their "highest selves." Enabling staff to see that delivering quality care contributes to peoples' lives, health and well being is your charge as a leader. Staff needs to observe in your leadership a consistent stand for excellence and absolute focus on patients (your customers) and on the business of dental health.

Now why did YOU stop asking for referrals? Leading by example — asking for referrals yourself — shows confidence in your practice and your staff to provide exceptional service. You can't expect them to ask if you aren't willing. Be a leader and lead the way. Model excellence and confidence and ask for referrals. Staff will follow.

My Coaching: Begin asking at staff meetings, "What are you getting out of asking patients to refer?" Manage the inquiry so staff sees the value — increased self-worth, greater confidence, more team spirit, better relations with you, etc. Use examples about the difference "they/we" are making by treating new patients. In this way, you will replace emergency with real value and a sense they are making a difference in peoples' lives. With these two elements in place, you'll be able to sustain the initiative.

ACCELERATING DECISIONS: THE SECRET KEY OF MARKETING

I tried Word of Mouth marketing in my office. My staff doesn't like doing it. I don't like doing it. It seems like more trouble than its worth. Tell me again why I should use word of mouth marketing as my primary marketing tool?

I still don't get why Word of Mouth marketing would be any more effective than my 1-800-Dentist, Yellow Pages or my radio spots. I also believe if we treat our patients right, a few will refer.

Why should I pursue Word of Mouth marketing any more than I am, when I am doing other marketing activities?

• • •

First, ask yourself what you are trying to do with your marketing. Put simply, you are trying to get people in your community to be new patients in your office. You are trying to get these people to be new patients in the most cost effective manner possible so you can generate the most profit.

Right now, I would guess you spend a lot on marketing and get very little profit from it. The fact is your ROI (return on investment) from your current marketing efforts is most likely abysmal.

There are four ways to increase profits related to marketing. The first three are what everyone talks about. The fourth is what I see as the most important, yet it's the one no one talks about. The first one is to increase the number of new patients that come to your office. Number two is to increase the dollar amount each new patient spends in your office. And number three is to increase the frequency with which new patients utilize your services. Marketing is supposed to achieve these three objectives. But in my view, 1-800-Dentist, Yellow Pages, Radio, TV, Billboards, Brochures, Websites, etc., are fairly weak in producing results. Worse, they all miss the most fundamental and critical aspect of effective marketing.

My assertion is that the most important way to increase new patients, thereby increasing revenues, is to "increase the speed with which decisions are made." Decision acceleration is the most powerful way to generate new patients and word of mouth marketing is definitely, far and away, the most powerful way to accelerate decisions.

Numerous articles have stated that approximately 50 percent of the population doesn't see a dentist on a routine basis. It doesn't mean they aren't considering it; it doesn't mean they aren't thinking about it; it doesn't mean they aren't concerned about it. Many of the people in this group are simply trying to decide what to do. So there is a vast market segment that is "deciding" about a dentist. Money, time, pain, embarrassment, afraid of being duped — all play a role in thwarting or stopping their decision to see a dentist.

The primary impact of word of mouth marketing is that it significantly increases *decision speed* — the time it takes a person to go from awareness or general concern to pulling the switch to be a new patient. So effective word of mouth marketing directly increases the decision process.

Suppose there are five dentists in your immediate neighborhood. All things being equal, you will capture a 20% market share. Say the decision cycle time for people to choose and see a dentist is about two years. Now suppose you find a way to make several of the tough steps in that decision cycle easier, cutting that decision time in half. What happens to your market share and your competitors' market share?

It is very clear that marketing success is determined much more by the time it takes a person to decide on seeing a dentist than any other single factor. If your word of mouth marketing decreases the decision time from two years to one year, then you will be able to capture another 20% of the market in the same time span.

This does not even touch on the powerful effect of word of mouth marketing and how it takes fence sitters and motivates them to act. And there is another benefit, when you increase decision speed by 100 percent, you not only get new patients, you get many more advocates for your services before your competitors have a similar opportunity. More patients are available sooner, your endorsements are supported by more people and the information (conversations) you provided to shorten the decision cycle are in place and working.

Choosing a dentist is not a single decision, it's a series of decisions. Some choices along the way can be fast and easy. "Is the dentist readily accessible and available? Does he or she honor my insurance? Is the dentist conveniently located? Other choices require much more time and effort in gathering and verifying information. They are bottlenecks in the decision process. They require consideration, weighing the options, testing and evaluating results and relationships. The process of deciding is slowed by each of these time-consuming bottlenecks.

In our Word of Mouth Marketing Program, we identify many of these bottlenecks and figure out how to minimize them so people can reduce their decision time. For example, one critical bottleneck we identify is the "risks" that patients take about going to a new dentist. This is a major bottleneck. We generate conversations we can have with potential patients or existing patients when speaking to friends, which addresses these risks. Risks such as the loss of time and money; will the dentist take advantage of me; will I be treated fairly; will he or she listen to me.

These communications can be delivered as 1) benefits, claims and promises, 2) testimony through existing patients, 3) easy trial offers, and 4) a way to demonstrate supportive, compassionate and caring relationships. These communications are part of Word of Mouth marketing and they significantly accelerate the decision process.

THREE MAGICAL INTERACTIONS THAT PRODUCE SUPERIOR CUSTOMER SERVICE

Competition is getting fierce. For the last seven years I was the only orthodontist in my immediate area, but last year, two new orthodontists moved in. They're undercutting me by pricing themselves much lower than my fees. I can't afford to compete at this fee level. My overhead is far too high, but I don't want to lay people off and I don't want to take a cut in salary either.

Over the last year, my new patients were down by 10%, my case acceptance was down by 15% and my revenues reflect this. I now have many more patients shopping for price. Worse, this downward trend line looks like it is going to continue if I don't do something.

What I see I can do is compete by providing significantly better customer service than my competition. Given my experience, my experienced staff, our clinical expertise, and my facility compared to my competition, I ought to be able to provide outstanding customer service and get us ahead once again.

What can I do immediately to improve customer service?

• ∘ •

Our research and our findings, especially over the last five years, where we used patient satisfaction surveys and parent-patient satisfaction surveys, clearly demonstrates three interactions that strongly and directly influence patients' perceptions of a dental office as having superior customer service.

First, our research demonstrates that those first few moments after a patient enters your office influences a patient's overall satisfaction more than any other service that follows. Malcolm Gladwell's book, *BLINK*, really makes this point well.

So the first place I'd look to enhance customer service is in how your patients are being greeted. What immediate impression does your office make? Are patients greeted immediately? Are patients greeted warmly?

Does the receptionist's desk face people who enter the office? Does the receptionist understand that her job is to make patients feel totally welcome and special? Are your phones always answered within three rings? Are your phones answered warmly? Is your office alive? Those first few moments are fundamental and critical.

Have friends call your office and report back how the phone was answered and how they were treated. Have a friend come into the office and let you know how they were greeted. This is essential for great customer service.

Second, our findings from hundreds of our patient satisfaction surveys point out what I call "Lesson of 24." We have found that offices that have a policy to follow up with patients within 24 hours of the their visit with a simple message have a 40 percent higher satisfaction rating than those offices that do not follow up.

"Is everything OK. Did you get the information/service you needed? Is there anything more we can provide for you?" Both staff members and doctor call patients — it is part of their job description. Follow up all patient visits within 24 hours. Always.

Finally, our research clearly demonstrated that sending hand written Thank You notes to patients who refer, accept significant treatment plans or have any significant contact with the office, makes a tremendous difference. These Thank You notes have the greatest impact if they are issued within five days of the interaction. Computer generated and printed notes are too easy to create from a template and easy to delegate to a staff member. Handwritten notes clearly show the patient, that he or she was worth your time. As a specialist, this is especially effective with your referring dentists.

To review, the recommendations for generating superior customer service immediately:

1. Create and manage your greetings of patients and parents so they exude warmth, affinity, kinship and caring.

2. Call all patients / parents after appointments within 24 hours.

3. Write handwritten notes to referring docs and parents within 5 business days.

Start these three activities immediately and you will immediately impact customer service.

THAT'S WHY THEY CALL IT FEE-FOR-SERVICE

I want out! Out of insurance. Out of PPOs. I can't stand it anymore — 20% write offs, waiting 90 to 120 days for my money, dancing to "their" tune, struggling all the time to get things approved. How do I make the leap? I want to be a totally fee-for-service dentist.

•　∘　•

I hear this refrain all the time. "I want to drop my participation with PPOs. I don't want to be a Delta provider anymore. I'm tired of writing off thousands of dollars. I'm frustrated having to argue with them on every claim. Who are they to set my fees? Who are they to tell me what kind of dentistry I can do? I'm angry getting paid 90 days after I deliver the dentistry."

Sound familiar?

I've never met a dentist who didn't want to be a pure fee-for-service dentist. Have you?

However, what dentists actually mean is not "fee-for-service" at all. What they really want when they say fee-for-service is "unregulated fee-for-dentistry." What most dentists imply by fee-for-service is "I want to set my own fees and have patient pay on or before the time the dentistry is delivered. And if the patient can't afford it, get the patient to secure credit. That's what dentists are talking about when they say "fee-for-service." The problem is most dentists don't really understand the "service" part.

What's missing is dentists actually doing what's needed to make the leap to a true fee-for-service practice. They grumble, "I really want to be a fee-for-service practice," but the problem is they haven't a clue how to provide the "service" for the fee. They have service confused with dentistry. Implants, crowns, scaling and root planning, porcelain inlays and veneers are not service, they are dental treatment.

If you want to become a fee-for-service practice, you will have to make genuine service the heart of your practice. You must understand that service creates real value for people. If you become a bona fide service provider, it will force you to reinvent yourself.

You need to appreciate and understand that outstanding service allows every employee to feel they can make a difference. You'll understand that great service is what people talk about since it is out of the ordinary. If you work hard to generate exceptional service, it will demand that you and your staff become outstanding performers. If you commit yourself to incomparable service, it will force you to become a much more powerful leader and manager. Are you willing to do that?

What I ordinarily find is most dentists are unwilling to change, take risks, make demands, or become rigorous about providing exceptional service. What they want is to continue what they are already doing, not change anything, and somehow just get paid full-fare with cash up-front. So if you really want to become a fee-for-service practice, first ask yourself, are you really willing to make those changes in yourself and your staff that will deliver extraordinary service to your patients?

Are you willing to fire people who might be technically competent but service incompetent? Are you willing to change your style, your hours, and your way of managing patients? Are you willing to invest substantial dollars into developing a service-oriented practice? If the answer is "No" to any of these questions, you're not ready to become a true fee-for-service practice since you won't be providing great service for the fee, just great dentistry.

Where do you begin to be a real fee-for-service practice? In our one day *Put Service in Fee-For-Service Workshop*, we begin by creating the context of service. To do this, you need to recognize where you are in regards to service at the moment the workshop begins. In order to generate the context, we reverse the order. Rather than be a fee-for-service practice, we ask you to examine your practice as a "service-for-fee" practice. What if the quality of service determined how much you got paid, how well would you do? Are you a Ritz-Carlton or a Motel 6?

On a scale of 1 to 10, how would you rate your quality of service today? Now imagine that a 1 would yield a $100,000 a year practice and a 10 would yield a $1 million a year practice. Well, how much money would you make a year as you are currently constituted? What would you need to do to become a 10 in service?

Next in the workshop we delve much more deeply into what is service, what is a powerful interpretation of service and what gets in the way of you serving others? When you get to understand what service is, what constitutes extraordinary service, then you need to decide and commit to making the necessary changes to be a "service-for-fee" practice or not.

There you have it. If you want to become a fee-for-service practice, put service in as the core of your practice. How to best define service? One of my teachers once said this about service: "When I don't know who I am, I serve you. When I know who I am, I am you." When you can totally and fully stand in another's shoes, then you can easily anticipate the other person's thinking, mood and wants. That's your first step in service.

If people have their attention on their jobs, their problems, their situations, they don't have the wherewithal to stand in another's shoes. Your job as a leader is to move them out of their heads and into the shoes of your patients.

When you and your staff can stand in the patient's shoes then you and your staff can fully anticipate what is wanted and needed for the patient to be totally satisfied. Once you can see with the patient's eyes, feel what the patient feels, it's just a matter of delivering what would make the biggest difference for the patient.

- Exceptional service will set your practice apart from your competition.

- Extraordinary service will have the community (market) talking about you.

- Outstanding service will directly increase new patient referrals from existing patients.

187

- Fabulous service will directly support team development and execution. A staff totally committed to extraordinary service will naturally be self-motivating and self-governing, greatly decreasing the necessity of your managing them.

THE ANSWER TO SETTING YOUR FEES

I am in my fourth year of practice. I purchased the practice and the senior dentist is now gone. I am trying to figure out how to determine my fees. I used the fee schedule that was in the practice when I bought it and simply raised it between 3-5 percent last year. A lot of how I determined my fees also had to do with me belonging to Delta and MetLife, which I no longer do.

My strategy is to keep my fees low, figuring that will attract more patients. My area is very competitive and there have been a lot of layoffs, so I believe keeping my fees low is one way to capture business.

What's your advice on setting your fees? Do you think it's a good idea to keep my fees low?

•   ⁕   •

Low fees do not boost business. In fact, low fees cost you business.

You need to understand that dentistry is basically an unregulated industry. You can charge as little or as much as you want. I've heard everything about setting fees; "my area," "what everyone else is charging," "location," "Delta," "usual and customary," "competition," "the economy is bad," "look at the price of gas."

But what if all these assumptions are misconceptions?

How else would you explain one dentist charging $1,700 per fixture for his implants and right down the block another dentist charging $2,800 for the same implant? And interestingly enough, the dentist who is charging $2,800 is a lot busier than the guy charging $1,700? Why? If low fees made the difference, how would you explain this occurrence?

Your belief that lower fees will boost business might not be true. Success in dental practice comes from good patients with strong, profit-producing fees. Trying to succeed by providing the lowest fees, pushes you under, not up. What happens when you pass a store that has plastered across its window, "Lowest Prices in Town"? What do you think about this store? Would you shop there or, if you do, how do you behave as a customer?

When you operate on the belief that the only way you can compete and succeed is by having low fees, what you're actually reinforcing is the reality that you can't make any real money in dental practice, the overhead is too high, the labor is too expensive, and people only want the cheapest prices. You are a victim of the myth that lower fees stimulate business. It's simply not true that dental patients only respond to your price.

The biggest fear you have when you start a dental practice is you're not going to make it. So the minute you start a practice, you are vulnerable to money fears. One component of the money fear is you slide into the "scarcity" mentality — you're afraid you might never make enough money.

So what do you do with any belief? You project that belief out into the external world. Part of the external world is your patients. "Look at them — see, they have money issues. They're scared of spending." When a patient declines treatment, your assumption is, "the only reason she didn't say 'Yes' was our prices were too high." But this conclusion is fear based and actually false. Anais Nin said it best; "We don't see things as they are, we see things as we are." If money is an issue for you — you make it an issue for your patients.

Does this sound familiar; "The reason I'm not getting enough new patients is because people in my community don't have enough money to spend on dentistry." Based on this perspective, you are only left with one solution to get new patients — keep fees low.

But what you are actually doing is projecting your struggles onto your patients. It's compounding the error. The patient isn't struggling with your fees — you just think so. Somehow you have to consider that lower prices are not the answer.

You've undoubtedly noticed as you drive by trailer parks and seen expensive pick-up trucks, large SUVs and huge satellite dishes. Makes you wonder. The only explanation is people will always spend money when it's a priority. People buy what they want and will pay whatever it costs. The thing to understand is not to give people what they can afford, it's to give them something they want.

So my advice is to change your focus. Focus on what patients want. Then focus on what you can add to address a further and deeper want. Then you are providing value. Value can and ought to be the determinant in setting your fees.

A bed in a hotel is a bed in a hotel, right?. Stay in a Holiday Inn Express and then stay at an Omni Hotel. The price is nearly double. Why? You are paying for value, the differences in the physicality, the service, the ambiance, the food, the quality of employees. All those elements increase value and that's what determines the price. And in my view, it's the same thing that determines your fees. Value.

You can keep your fees climbing higher right along with increasing the value for the patient. By focusing on value, you can convert from a "low price" focus to a "strong price" focus. The truth that people pay for what they want will be evident — and the truth shall set you free.

Now if I were consulting you, I would suggest that you immediately raise your fees by 11-15 percent. But there is one condition. You must also increase the value at least the same amount, if not more.

Focus on raising value and then raising your fees feels fully justified. In other words, the higher level of value you generate for the patient, the higher level of fee you can charge, and actually feel good about it.

Value can be generated in two ways. One is intrinsically, where you feel your work is more valuable. This increase in value is achieved through continued training and development in care delivery. You would need to spend money, time and effort in your professional development. Kois, Spears, Pankey, and others are but a few paths you could follow to increase the intrinsic value for patients.

The second way of increasing value is extrinsic, and in many ways is just as important as improving the level and quality of dentistry delivered. But more often than not, this domain of value is rarely addressed in dental practice. Extrinsic value shows up in everything and everywhere the practice touches the patient. From the reception area to the confirmation calls. From the kind of stationary you use to the kind of toilet paper in your bathrooms.

But how often do you and your staff talk about upgrading value for your patients? How many times do you ask, "How do we improve value for the patient in the practice?" Is it even talked about at all?

From my point of view, the ultimate determinant of your fees is value. Provide a very high value experience and high level of dentistry for your patients and you can legitimately charge higher fees and feel good about it. What you will also discover is you will attract lots of high quality patients.

DON'T BE A "CHOOVIDER"

Every time I have to present an expensive treatment plan, I back down and either don't present it or say it in a way that the patient thinks it's a dream-like option. I always end up somewhere toward the least expensive treatment.

For example, I see a five surface amalgam with a cusp that soon will fracture and rather than strongly recommending a crown, I say "Let's wait and see."

Why can't I make strong treatment plan recommendations? Why do I always punk out?

• ◦ •

You need to understand something and you need to get it down to your toes. The patient is the chooser, you are the provider. They are distinct. They are different. Each, the chooser and the provider, have roles to play. Each has their own duties to perform. Each has a different set of intentions, interests and concerns.

You, like many dentists are collapsing the two. The chooser is the chooser and the provider is the provider — get it straight. You have morphed them into one — the "choovider." You do this by thinking the patient is like you. You do this by believing the patient is coming from the same concerns, issues and problems as you. You think you can read their minds. Wake up. You are not the patient. You are the dentist!

The patient is totally capable of making their own choices. Your job is to make offers for them to choose from, not to choose for them. They know their situation a lot better than you. They know their needs and wants better than you. They know their priorities better than you. You are not there to decide for them. You are there to put them in a position to decide. You are there to empower them to make a choice.

Your job is to provide information that allows them to appropriately consider the choices, the outcomes from the choices and the consequences that come with each choice.

Choice is the forerunner of responsibility. Responsibility promotes commitment. Committed action is far more effective and produces more reliable results. I think you would prefer to work on committed patients. Committed patients make their appointments and pay their bills. Committed patients refer other patients. Committed patients are easy to manage and somehow the dental work always turns out better.

Many consultants can provide you with techniques to manipulate patients into saying "Yes." It's pure sales. I prefer you open your interactions with a new patient and tell them it's going to be up to them to make some choices and to make choices that work for them. Choices they can be committed to carrying out.

You'll give them your professional perspective. You'll give them ample information. You will outline the consequences of each choice, since every choice has a consequence. They'll know the upside and downside of each choice. But you will not decide for them. Only they can decide for themselves.

Begin with what you honestly believe and stand for as the best treatment for this case. Tell them why you believe it. Tell them why you'd do this for yourself if it were your mouth. Ask if they understand your recommendations and why.

Now, go down the list of options until you reach "no treatment." At each step ask if they understand the treatment and the consequences — the upside and downside of each treatment proposed.

Review the choices. Ask them if they have any questions or concerns that have come up or they need addressed. Now, ask them to choose.

There will be a moment of silence and discomfort. Be patient with it. Don't force it. Don't start explaining again. Don't give them the "I understand how hard this is for you" story. They are in the midst of making a choice — and with that choice, comes the consequences of money, time and outcome.

When you realize the patient is the chooser and not you, it removes the burden from you of having to convince the patient. It also empowers you to operate with and inside integrity. It promotes honesty, authenticity and straight-talk. It changes your context from a commodity peddler to a service provider.

The patient either will or they won't. It's their choice. It's not up to you, it's up to the patient — and that's the way it should be.

LOYALTY BEYOND REASON

It's bad and getting worse. I've been in practice 12 years. My production and new patients are dwindling. Patients are leaving. Competition is increasing. Five new dentists in the last two years.

The reasons patients tell me they are leaving are: 1) I am not on their panel list, 2) I don't take their insurance, or 3) I'm too expensive. Things have gotten so bad I am considering signing up for a number of plans and just eating the discount. I feel that's the only thing I can do.

Worse, I spent the last few years training with John Kois. I want to practice top-of-the-line dentistry, but with my patients leaving like they are, it looks like I'll never be able to have a high-end restorative practice.

What should I do?

• • •

I hear this concern a lot. "Patients are leaving because of insurance," or "patients are leaving because of the expense." From my perspective, you are not using this breakdown of patients exiting to create a better future. Rather, you are using this breakdown as an "excuse" to not produce results. You are speaking like a victim and victims get victimized.

Your interpretation of this situation greatly reduces your power and devalues who you are. Your interpretation of why patients are leaving you leaves you weak and unable to succeed. Your interpretation of why people are leaving results in you thinking there is nothing you can do to stop the bleeding and you've got little power in reversing the trend. That's the totally wrong path to go down. My coaching is "Stop it now!"

Kevin Roberts in his book, *Lovemarks*, suggests you generate *loyalty beyond reason*. This works well with brands and retail, but how do you generate patients who have *loyalty beyond reason* to your practice? Loyalty that isn't based on money or insurance?

First, look in your own life. You have particular relations with people that are not based on reason. Identify those very special relationships in which you have *loyalty beyond reason*, where time, money or convenience is never in the way. What's available in these relationships that delivers this kind of unconditional loyalty? Take your relationship with Dr. Kois. Is your relationship based on economics? Does cost affect your decision? How about time, travel, and convenience? I doubt it. What is present in your relationship with John that has you be loyal beyond reason?

I would say that a particular aspect of why you are loyal to John is he sees you as how you want to be seen. He holds you as your highest thought about yourself. He totally believes in what he is doing and knows that if you believe in it too, you will succeed. Who he is for you, is who you want to be.

Can you be that for your staff and your patients? Can you be an unconditional stand for the dentistry you provide? If you feel hypocritical or pretentious about what you're offering patients, it won't work. You need to be totally genuine, authentic, real about what you can do for your patients. You need to be able to deliver on what you promise your patients. If you can do that, then you have a fighting chance to retain your patients and even expand your patient base.

This will also have a direct impact on your staff. If you become the dentist that patients will be loyal to, then so will your staff. They will also become *loyal beyond reason.*

Patient who are *loyal beyond reason* rarely if ever miss their appointments, they pay their bills on time, are happy to see you, glad you're their dentist, refer new patients whenever they can, and promote you to their neighbors and coworkers.

If you can uncover that fire for your dentistry, a true intent to do the best for the patient, then you wouldn't be worried about insurance or money, because it would be a molehill, not a mountain. You need to be the person, in thinking, action and being that people will be *loyal to without reason.*

MEASURE WHAT PATIENTS WANT, NOT WHAT YOU WANT

I have been in practice 11 years. At first, my rate of growth was explosive — double digits for the first five years. But over the last few years, my growth has slowed until last year I didn't grow at all. How can I reignite dynamic growth in my practice?

• · •

If mature dental practices were granted a single wish, just like you, their most frequent request would surely be for a reliable way to create new growth. What has worked in the past no longer has the same punch.

When I first engage established practitioners in increasing practice growth, they often ask; "Do I continue to do what I've always done in the past? Or do I take a leap and try something new and radical?" The answer is neither. Don't change what you do, change what you measure.

You see, what you have to do is change your perspective and that will change everything. To change your perspective, change what you measure.

Begin to change what you measure by asking yourself the question, what is valuable to my patients? Now I'm not talking about whiter teeth or better breath, although these things are valuable to patients. I am talking about other features of the way you run your practice and what patients value.

Here's an example. Patients value timeliness. Being seen on time. Being dismissed on time. Nobody likes to wait. Nobody. Yet most practices don't measure being on time. How about if you measured being on time? When patients are not seen within 5 minutes of their appointed time, it gets noted on the schedule. At the end of the week, take the number of times you were late for patients, divided by the total number of appointments that week and that would produce a percentage of being late for patients.

Each column would be measured (dentist, hygienists and assistants if applicable) and how often they are late. The practice develops a weekly score generated in percentages, i.e. Dentist A is late 24% of the time. Then targets are set. Dentist A will improve his on-time-ness by 10% over the next three weeks. Dentist A meets with his team, they discuss how to improve performance and then they continue to measure.

Players in every industry settle on common units of measurement. With lawyers it's billable time. With consumer goods producers it's sales of cereal or bars of soap. With the airline industry it's passenger trips. Each industry has its standard units of measurement — the fundamental unit of measuring units of business — a way to assess the success of the transaction between buyer and seller. In dentistry it happens to be production, collection, new patients and case acceptance.

Associated with each set of these measures, usually called "key metrics," there are other measures to assess how well a company or practice is doing with respect to profitability. In the airline industry an example would be cost per passenger mile flown and seat yield. In a dental practice examples would be overhead percentage or production per hour per provider.

But what you notice about all these measurements, the common units of measurement (key metrics) and measurements related to profitability, is they all have to do with the performance of the practice and little to do with increasing value for the patient.

One way to grow your business is to begin to measure other areas of the practice that generate value for your market (patients). Measure those things that reflect value creation for your patients. Measure your performance in areas that patients really care about. But be aware, when you change the way and what you measure, it will have a far reaching impact on the entire practice.

Take the example above, measuring patients being seen on time. Well that simple measurement will change everything. How the patient is interacted with on the phone — so they show up on time. How the assistants clean and set up the rooms — so they can be seated on time. How the dentist honors her time and keeps her word — doesn't overextend him or herself to do more. How the patient is dismissed. How the patient is confirmed before their next appointment. This one measure, being on time, will change how the entire practice operates.

The real beauty of measuring what patients' value is you will be much more focused on what patients appreciate than just on how the practice is performing. In measuring what patients appreciate, your business processes and, if you want, your incentives, will be much more aligned with what patients and the market cares about.

How you determine what aspects of the practice to create new metrics is to examine where patients perceive problems or unfulfilled expectations in the practice. Being seen on time is certainly one, but there are plenty of others. Then, figure out how to measure these areas, set goals and then improve your performance in these areas. Anywhere from measuring speed of filing patients' insurance, answering phones in three rings or less, conveniently confirming appointments.

By measuring what patients' value, you'll enhance the patient experience. Case acceptance will go up. Word of mouth marketing will increase. And the practice will be focused on actions that will get you and the staff energized about the practice as you were when you first started practice. Any way you can expand value for the patient, measure your performance in these areas, and then your practice will begin to grow once again.

BREAKING THROUGH EXCUSES

I am very frustrated and sometimes depressed about my practice. After 13 years I am not doing very well. First of all, I just can't find good staff. I've put ads in the paper, talked to colleagues, talked to local dental headhunters, but there aren't any good candidates available. Maybe I can't recruit good staff because I can't pay them very well, at least as well as my more successful peers.

I can't get the staff I do have to really care about the practice or operate like a team. They aren't really committed to the practice and don't seem to be concerned about whether we are successful or not.

I'm also not getting enough new patients. I think this is because of our location and the fact we really don't know how to market. I'd like to do some marketing but I don't have the money because my cash flow is really weak. I can hardly pay myself, yet alone afford to do marketing.

When I do get patients, I can't get them to go for the higher quality care. I am pretty sure this is because I am in a lower-end area with mostly blue collar workers who are all on dental insurance with low dental IQs.

How do I overcome these terrible circumstances to have a successful practice?

•　∘　•

You have an excuse for staff under-performing. You have an excuse for poor revenue production. You have an excuse for lack of new patients. You even have an excuse for having excuses.

Excuses are reasons — your reasons for non-performance and your reasons for poor results. In business, you either have your reasons or you have results. You need to stop making excuses for why you can't get it done — and get it done.

Why would you need the ability to generate excuses for why it's impossible to do things everyone agrees are important? I recently made a presentation to a large study club. The topic was how to increase staff loyalty and performance. I was barely 20 minutes into the presentation when a dentist raised his hand and gave me all the reasons why it couldn't be done. Why am I not surprised? I hear the same thing about budgets, office policies, performance reviews, targets, asking for new patients. The list goes on and on.

Excuses impede change. Without change, you fail to improve. You lose out to other dentists who see challenges as something to be surmounted. After all, patients will be happy to switch dentists that fix problems rather than complain about them.

Here's how to stop making excuses and start getting things done.

1) *Do not accept preemptive surrender.*
   Don't give up before you start. Stop rationalizing the status quo. Stop coming up with reasons why it can't be done. Examples of common excuses can easily be found in doing and managing by a budget:

   "I don't have a budget because 1) I don't have the time, 2) I'm not good with numbers, 3) I don't understand how to do one, 4) my accountant gives me a P & L so why do I need one, and/or 5) even if I knew what I spent my money on, what could I really do about my expenses." These are only the tip of this iceberg of excuses about budgets.

2) *Articulate the benefits of moving beyond extraordinary excuses and find extraordinary solutions.*
   Here's an example; "I can't get my hygienist to be a team player because 1) she is a Prima-Donna, 2) hygienists are hard to find, 3) patients really like her, 4) I don't want to confront her because she gets angry and resentful, 5) she came with the practice and knows all the patients, and/or 6) she does a really good job with patients." An extraordinary solution would be "I will have a heart-to-heart interaction with my hygienist this week, lay it on the line, and if she doesn't improve her team play, I'll let her go."

3) *Demolish excuses by example.*
   Here's an example: "We don't ask for new patients because 1) it's embarrassing, 2) it feels like sales, 3) I don't know how to do it, 4) what if the patient thinks I'm desperate, 5) patients don't

want to refer, or 6) I don't want to look needy." The dentist should get over it and start asking patients for new patients. Set an example for his or her staff. Stop giving excuses why he or she can't. Be brave. Be courageous. Stop being a wimp-puppy. Ask patients to refer their friends and family.

One thing you notice immediately in people who make excuses is in their language. They use "because" and "but" in most of their sentences. (Re-read your own e-mail.) Anything that follows a "because" or a "but" is the reason why it can't or won't get done. Furthermore, whatever follows "because" or "but" takes the speaker off the hook and makes another person or circumstance the reason why it won't happen. Ultimately, "because" and "but" removes you from being responsible and makes someone else or something else responsible.

Excuses drag a dental practice toward an unprofitable, dissatisfying end. Your job is to counteract excuses. If you don't, you and your staff can trade excuses all day about why you keep on failing.

CALENDAR & CHECKBOOK

How do I get my staff to provide excellent customer (patient) service?

I am totally committed to excellent customer service. I understand how it gives me a real competitive edge. I understand how it enhances patients referring new patients and increases case acceptance. I know that in a fee-for-service practice how critical patient service and patient satisfaction really are.

What's the answer here?

• • •

Please excuse me for saying this, but I don't believe you. Nope. Not a word. I think you're full of it.

I don't believe you when you say "I am totally committed to excellent customer (patient) service." I'm willing to bet you're like most dentists and like most dentists you don't walk the talk, but you sure as heck talk the talk.

Yes, I know you say that you are unconditionally committed to superior patient service. I know you say you are totally committed to the highest level of patient satisfaction. But, commitment shows up in two places, your calendar and your checkbook.

Let me see your calendar for the last six months and how much time was scheduled for you and your staff to address patient satisfaction and service. How much per day, per week, per month?

Let me look at your CE and consulting calendar for the last 12 months. How much time did you schedule for training and education in improving patient service and satisfaction?

In the area of service, let me see what you measure on a daily, weekly and monthly basis. Any place you're truly committed, you are measuring. What areas of patient service and satisfaction are you measuring? Be specific.

My bet is you spend little if any time or money on patient service and satisfaction. My bet is you measure zip in these areas. My bet is you spend very little time on educating, training and developing yourself and your staff to deliver excellent patient service and satisfaction. My bet is you talk the talk and fail to walk the talk.

If patient service were truly fundamental and critical to you, you'd be measuring various areas of patient satisfaction. You'd be running patient satisfaction surveys. You'd be questioning your patients about your service and responding to their answers on a regular basis.

How many patients did you personally call last week to talk about your service and their satisfaction? Did the conversation go something like; "Thank you, Mrs. Jones, for being a patient in our office. How satisfied are you? Will you continue to use our services? Is there anything you'd like to tell me — good or bad?" How many patients did you call? Zero? When it doesn't show up on your calendar and in your checkbook it's just a lot of hot air.

My coaching is straightforward about this: simply commit totally to patients being completely satisfied. You see, being satisfied is OK, but completely satisfied is the goal. My assertion is a completely satisfied patient is three times more likely to refer new patients, accept treatment recommendations and pay their bills on time, than a patient who is just satisfied.

Now if you want to make "completely satisfied" part of your culture, you'll figure out a way to incorporate patient satisfaction ratings into your pay-raise policy. That would boost staff's intention and attention to patients being completely satisfied. For example, if the practice didn't score 95 or above in patient satisfaction surveys for the year, no raises period - and that would include you.

If on one of your patient exit interviews, patient satisfaction surveys or Web interactions, a patient said, "I really liked Jill who really took care of me, she was just terrific," two things happen. First, that compliment gets reported the next day so Jill knows that she did a great job and a patient said something nice about her. Two, if these compliments are consistent, they carry a lot of weight to getting some higher level of compensation either as a bonus of some type of a raise in salary at her next review.

Likewise, if someone said that the way they were greeted was not very pleasant, that also gets reported the next day and real action, no nonsense action, for correction would take place. And if it happens repeatedly, there would be very real consequences. Is that the way you now operate?

If patient service and satisfaction were critical, you would hire people who interact with patients in such a way as to have them completely satisfied. Before you put them to work, you'd spend time making sure they understand that patients being completely satisfied is job one. You would explain to them what's really important to your patients — information derived from exit interviews, phone calls, and surveys. You'd tell them that all raises and promotions, in large part, are based on patient satisfaction and service.

But I suspect that the only criteria for hiring is to see if the individual can get their job done, be compatible with other staff members, ask for pay within the pay range you are considering, and not cause you any trouble. Would I be right?

As I said, most dentists are windbags when it comes to patient service and satisfaction. How do I know? I simply ask to see their checkbook and their calendar. That's how I know. When I ask a dentist what he or she measures on a routine basis, I invariably hear production, collection, new patients, and occasionally case acceptance. I sometimes hear that he or she measures recall return rates and expense-spending but, I rarely if ever hear, "I measure patient satisfaction."

If it's true that in business and life you get what you measure, what does the absence of measuring patient service excellence and patient satisfaction tell you?

Having spent many years in organizational consulting with Fortune 1000 companies, I saw the power of measuring customer satisfaction. Some companies with whom I worked were nearly fanatical about it, others more moderate. But they all measured customer satisfaction. All! Customer service was critical to their businesses.

Since many dentists said they were absolutely and categorically committed to patient service, we created an online tool they could use to accurately measure patient satisfaction. The survey reveals what they are doing that is working and what they are doing that is not working in patient service. We generated reports of findings so dentists could get immediate and accurate feedback. We even provided a post survey phone consult to go over the results with the dentist. We were the "only game in town" for easy to use, accurate, patient satisfaction surveys.

Almost ten years later, less than 1% of dentists use it.

THE MASTERY COMPANY

We don't work from the outside in. We work from the inside out. Our years of experience, our successes and our failures, have taught us that it's much more about WHO you are than WHAT you know or even what you do.

Systems, structures, protocols, budgets, employee manuals, job descriptions, flow charts, goals, and targets are important. And we provide these materials and models with our programs. But if that were all dentists needed to be successful, a lot more dentists would be successful. That's what makes our work so unique. We know that success begins within you.

Using our proven coaching and consulting technologies, we are able to transform who you are so that you become a commanding leader, a highly effective manager, a powerful owner and a great marketer. If you're already good, we'll make you great. If you're already great, we will make you even better.

THAT'S WHAT MAKES OUR WORK SO POTENT.

TOO GOOD TO BE TRUE,
BUT IT IS TRUE

I am considering hiring a practice management consultant. Nearly all of the consultants I am previewing cost between $25,000 and $40,000 for a one-year program. I've talked to my peers, and those who use you, swear by you.

However, your costs are so much less than all the others. This makes me very suspicious. You know what they say, "If it's too good to be true, it's too good to be true." Why is there such a discrepancy in cost between you and the other practice management consultants?

• • •

Thanks for asking. I love this question!

Business is business. Your dental practice is a business. What are the ends any business owner wants to achieve? Improve their top and bottom line. Have greater peace, grace and ease in recruiting, retaining and managing employees. Have a robust infrastructure that guides and deftly directs the business. Have greater certainty in decision making in critical areas to improve performance. Develop a keen ability to foresee the future and invent strategy and tactics to meet it. Generate abilities to handle conflicts and reduce upsets. Enhance competitive competencies to continually succeed in their market. Continuously improve their abilities as an owner, leader, manager and marketer. Increase the asset value of the business for higher resale value. All these are universal ends of any business. My job is to educate, train and develop dentists to achieve these ends.

However, the "means" to produce these ends is a whole other story.

Knowing the ends of any business, and having consulted numbers of businesses besides dental practices, including IT, software and Internet companies, I recognized early that digitization can dramatically reduce costs. Today, you can make local and long distance calls at no cost with Skype. You can book your own travel and save hundreds of dollars using Priceline.com or Travelocity.com. JetBlue, Men's Warehouse, Wal-Mart and IKEA use state of the art technologies that significantly reduce their costs structure and thus can profit from lower costs. New technologies can be used to crush costs and that's what we've done.

Here are a few examples. Ten years ago, it would cost us around $400 to write, publish and mail a monthly newsletter. Now we create a no-cost, no subscription fee, high-volume electronic newsletter on a weekly basis. Just as important, we get immediate feedback from readers, allowing us to better understand our market and their needs.

We used to offer practice/business assessments; traveling to dental offices, interviewing staff and dentists to find out what was going on. Five years ago our company developed a suite of user-friendly, scientifically valid online surveys and assessments; from staff performance reviews to staff satisfaction surveys, from patient satisfaction surveys to associate performance reviews. With these online tools we can now generate a powerful assessment of what is actually occurring in the practice. Again, this saves the client thousands of dollars since there is no travel/direct costs for the consultant and no down time for the practice. Just point and click.

Four years ago we developed an online budget and employee policy manual that our clients can easily reformat, edit to fit their office and then capture to their hard drive. We assist clients in developing strategic plans in PowerPoint which they can present to staff and peers and upgrade on a routine basis.

My primary consulting program, *Mastery of Practice,* used to be delivered in hotel meeting rooms with five 1½-day sessions, each session occurring 6 to 8 weeks apart. In today's dollars, given travel, direct costs and materials, the program would be priced at around $39,000 per participant. The Mastery program is now delivered totally electronically via e-mail, our exclusive Website technology, online surveys and assessments. The coaching and education is delivered via private 30-minute coaching calls and group conference calls each month. The program produces better and more sustained results for the client, at half the cost of the lower end of your range. We will be starting our 20th online Mastery program soon — guess that's the best validation of the success of our technology.

By using our own intranet, we continually consolidate information into available knowledge to constantly innovate new ways in cost reductions for both our clients and ourselves. All our backroom functions are automated, saving hundreds of hours and tons of money. These saving are then passed onto our clients. In 1994, I had a staff of seven, an expensive office in Seattle, Washington, and lots of paper. Today I have a staff of one, no office and we are paperless. Through digitization, automation and a robust Website we have reduced many consulting costs to near oblivion.

Unlike most other consultants, we don't have any "brick and mortar" to support. No pseudo-schools, no edifices, no two to five story glass and steel architectural structures to carry. We don't have numbers of support people to pay. We don't have multiple lines of business to fund and manage. We avoid political shenanigans. We make no attempt to get our picture on the cover of dental rags. We don't have any consultants to support and manage. We have no desire to "dominate" the industry. We have no desire to be the biggest. Our only desire is to be the best.

In our view, a client would prefer not to hassle with travel, get on airplanes, travel hundreds of miles, spend nights in a hotel room, but rather simply pick up the phone in their private office for a couple of 30-minute calls a month and then go home. Our belief is a client would choose to have a full day of production over sitting in some dark seminar room for a few days with 50 other dentists he doesn't know. Our assertion is our clients are self-governing and self-managing. They can learn the material and do the work from our assigned readings, downloads from our Website and e-mails, working on their computers from the office or home — in their own time. Our notion is a client would prefer to sit around a speaker phone at lunch-time with his or her staff rather than have some consultant come in for a day or dragging his entire staff to some hotel for a day and paying them their full day's salary.

Coupling technology with low overhead has proven a great business strategy. You need not look very far to see many examples of the success of this strategy. Ameritrade reduced their overhead by relocating to Nebraska, where real estate prices, local taxes and salary demands are extremely low. Ameritrade's Internet $9.95 trade price continues to show it is very profitable and the company is making it miserable for giant Morgan Stanley, where their key operations are located in expensive New York and San Francisco.

We have adopted this same business strategy. We've been working at it for years. And we know in our own small way, we're making it miserable for Mercer, Blatchford, Levine, Heartland and others. We don't have a large overhead to pass on to clients. We are always accessible and available electronically. And we are Web-centric so all the materials are located on our exclusive Website.

We can deliver top-of-the-rank consulting for much less than other consultants, and produce incredible results for clients without them leaving their office. In my view, we can deliver the wisdom of the ages through today's technology and produce noteworthy outcomes for clients at a third or fourth of the cost. In fact, we were named a Top Ten Finalist for the prestigious Dell Award for the business who uses technology to totally transform its industry and enhance the customer experience.

Now we realize our consulting technology and methods aren't for everyone but for many dentists it's a darn good fit. I hope that answered your question and addressed your concern.

And again, thanks for asking.

COACHING MAKES THE DIFFERENCE

I am a 47-year-old general practitioner. Two people in my local study club are in the Mastery of Practice program. They have really improved their production, staff performance and, more important, their moods. Those guys have done lots of practice management programs before, have had consultants and have spent lots of time on their businesses. But until recently, nothing has made much of a difference. Now they are doing gang-busters. When I ask why they are doing so well, they say, "Coaching."

What are they talking about? Can you tell me more?

• • •

Pavarotti can't hear himself sing. Tiger Woods can't see himself swing. Andy Roddick can't see himself hit the tennis ball. All professionals know that to improve performance, you need a coach.

Coaching involves a particular kind of relationship and a particular kind of intention. The relationship between a coach and his or her players is special and specific. Both are committed to the players' best performance. Both are committed to winning. Both are committed to team victory. And all of that takes place inside performance's being clearly defined by measurable outcomes and accomplishments.

A coach provides a committed partnership, something dentists generally lack in their practices. Dentists almost always go it alone. They pretend that things are working. They ignore the business side of their practices, claiming, "Everything is fine." But considering the variance in dental practice, where some practitioners have personal incomes well above $350K a year, but most have incomes far below that, everything is not fine — especially for those on the lower end of the scale.

How does coaching work? A coach empowers you to do those things that must be done. The things you always avoid doing or are afraid to do. For example, confronting an underperforming staff member. Asking patients for referrals. Generating a budget and managing by it. Developing a strategic plan and measuring yourself against it. Calling vendors about overdue supplies. Setting targets and goals. Getting charts done. Having a straight conversation with your lab. Having a difficult conversation with your associate. You get the point?

A coach interacts with you from the point of view that you can deliver, rather than the one you often look at yourself from, which is that you can't deliver. A coach provides a driving intention for you to stop procrastinating and get those things done that ensure the success of your business. A coach is a pain in your backside about doing the right thing. A coach doesn't buy your excuses. A coach doesn't buy your victim, villain or hopelessness stories.

When we do our surveys — during and after the Mastery course — 96% of the participants say coaching is the most valuable aspect of the program. As one participant put it: "The best part of the program was the coaching. Your coaching had me confront those areas that I had been avoiding. Your coaching had me take actions I knew I needed to take but was reluctant to take. Your coaching pushed me to take risks and get things done. I know that my recent accomplishments were my doing, but it was the coaching that allowed me to accomplish them."

How do you find a coach for yourself? First, you begin by asking for coaching. If you aren't asking for it, coaching shows up as a bother, an intrusion, an annoyance. I never coach people unless they have requested it. That's the first lesson I learned 25 years ago.

Second, you need to have a relationship with a coach of trust, affinity and kinship — and you must directly experience that those qualities truly exist. You need to feel in your gut that he or she is committed to your success. The coach is going to ask you to do things that you won't want to do, and if the relationship isn't in place, you won't do them.

Third, a good coach has a track record. Good coaches have coached players and teams to winning records — consistently. They know how to get the best out of their players. They also know that every player is different and has his or her own individual needs, strengths and weaknesses.

Fourth, a coach allows you to see differently. Through his or her relationship and communication, a coach allows you to see the field — your practice

— so that you are able to play better. Through your interactions with a coach, you also see yourself differently — you "see your own eyes" — and, therefore, can make corrections.

There are lots of people out there who take on the moniker of "coach." Yet, in my view, there are few who have the background of experience, the background of success and the skill set to really coach. If you are interested, do your due diligence. Ask questions. Do interviews. You know the routine. Find a coach who will get the best out of you and who you are certain is totally committed to your success.

Then again, there are a lot of dentists who don't want a coach. Some think they can do it alone, that they don't need anyone else. To me that's arrogant. They'd rather have their reasons than their results. They'd rather be right than happy. When you invite a coach into your world, you are asking for someone to confront, push and enable you to generate high performance that produces results. A coach will require you to change and, as you know, change is uncomfortable and risky. Most dentists would rather be comfortable, even though it isn't giving them what they want. And most dentists want to avoid taking risks. So, be aware that getting a coach will disrupt your comfort and push you to take risks. Are you ready for that?

DR. MARC COOPER

President, The Mastery Company
mcooper@emisar.com
www.TheMasteryCompany.com

Dr. Cooper is President and CEO of The Mastery Company. He has been a consultant to the health care industry for nearly 25 years — at the practice management level as well as at corporate and organizational levels. Prior to his consulting career, Dr. Cooper was an academician, basic science researcher and practicing periodontist.

His consulting clients have included more than 2,000 dentists practicing in solo, partnered and group practices and their corresponding support staffs. Dr. Cooper has also worked with senior executives, managers and supervisors in large health care systems, regional and community hospitals, third-party payers, clearinghouses, biotechnical firms, information technology companies, IPAs, PPOs, DPMs and DHMOs.

Dr. Cooper focuses the majority of his work on dentists in private practice, training and coaching them to achieve mastery as leaders, managers and owners who are able to consistently operate their dental practices as successful businesses.

ORDER FORM

Fax Orders: (603) 720-0369. Send this completed form.
Telephone Orders: Call (425) 806-8830. Have your credit card ready.
Postal Orders: Sahalie Press, PO Box 1806, Woodinville, WA 98072
Online Orders: Available Online at http://www.amazon.com
Email Contact: metrix@emisar.com

Please send the following books, disks or reports. I understand that I may return any item for a full refund — for any reason, no questions asked.

☐ *Mastering the Business of Practice* ($19.95)
☐ *SOURCE: The Genesis of Success in Business and Life* ($14.95)
☐ *Partnerships in Dental Practice: Why Some Succeed, Why Some Fail* ($14.95)
☐ *Running on Empty: Answers to Questions Dentists Have about the Recession* ($14.95)
☐ Subscription to the **Mastery Newsletter** (FREE)

Name: _____

Shipping Address: _____

City: _____

State: _____ **Zip Code:** _____

Sales Tax: Add 8.9% sales tax for products shipped to Washington addresses.

Shipping: $5.00 US for first book adn $2.00 US each additional book.

Payment: ☐ Personal Check
             ☐ Credit Card (Visa, MasterCard or Amex)

Card Number: _____ **Exp:** _____

Name on Card: _____

Billing Address if different from Shipping Address above:

_____

_____

_____

Made in the USA
San Bernardino, CA
07 October 2013